The Legends of Notts County

Dave Bracegirdle

breedon **books**
PUBLISHING

First published in Great Britain in 2005 by
The Breedon Books Publishing Company
Limited
Breedon House, 3 The Parker Centre,
Derby, DE21 4SZ.

ISBN 1 85983 463 9

Printed and bound by BIDDLES LTD,
King's Lynn, Norfolk.

Contents

Acknowledgements

A great debt of thanks is due to so many wonderful people, who helped in the creation and publication of *The Legends of Notts County*.

First and foremost, a huge thank you to the hundreds of supporters who emailed in with suggestions of players to be included. Among them were several friends and relatives with personal anecdotes of some of the legends that have been included.

My thirst for additional knowledge was always quenched by the ever-helpful Richard Stanton, David McVay, Colin Slater and Martin Shaw, who interrupted their own busy schedules to help out time after time.

Tracking down some of the former Magpies was made much easier by the willing assistance given by David Needham – or to be precise, his daughter Gabrielle and mum Betty.

The *Nottingham Evening Post* has covered all of County's highs and lows over the years and I am extremely grateful to Phillip Meakin, who supplied many of the photographs, and Paul Taylor, the Notts correspondent, for their invaluable help with this project.

Additional photographs are courtesy of Paul Wain, whom I would like to thank for all his help.

Thanks also to Mark Stevenson at Notts County, one of the most helpful press officers in the land, and to Steve Caron and Susan Last at Breedon Books for their continued faith and expertise.

As always, love and thanks to my partner Karen for her devoted support and patience. Finally, the biggest thank you goes to all the players, officials and personalities that have been included – I just hope that I have been able to accurately portray your story.

I hope you all enjoy *The Legends of Notts County*.

Dave Bracegirdle, August 2005

Harry Adamson

Date of birth: 27 June 1924, Kelty, Fife

Died: 23 May 1997

Notts County record:

Appearances: League 233, FA Cup 16

Goals: League 5, FA Cup 0

Debut: 17 April 1948 v Norwich City (h) lost 1–2

Also played for: Jeanfield Swifts, Gainsborough Trinity, Wisbech Town

Harry Adamson provided magnificent service to Notts County for almost a decade. In the immediate post-war years, the youngster had played junior football in Scotland before arriving in Nottingham to try his luck with the Magpies.

A willing runner, the stockily-built midfielder went on to compile almost 250 first-team appearances for the Magpies. After 18 months of reserve-team football, manager Arthur Stollery gave Harry his League debut towards the end of the 1947–48 campaign. The following season Harry began to establish himself in a side containing household names such as Tommy Lawton and Jackie Sewell. Both of those players hit four goals apiece in January 1951 as Newport County were beaten 11–1, County's highest winning margin in a Football League match. Although the 'big two' took the plaudits, each took time to congratulate and thank Harry, who had set up so many of the opportunities.

Just two weeks after that huge victory, Notts went down to a 1–0 defeat in the fourth round of the FA Cup but not before they had worried Liverpool, at Anfield, in front of over 61,000 people. Harry's dominating presence in the midfield did much to stifle the Merseysiders' attacking ambitions.

During the 1949–50 Division Three South championship season, Harry Adamson was one of only two players to play in every match – goalkeeper Roy Smith was the other. To this point in his career Harry had failed to register a single League goal, but he duly delivered on 21 April 1951 with the decider in a five-goal thriller at home to Swansea Town. This was a rare high spot in a disappointing season for the Scot, which was restricted to just 14 matches because of injury.

Harry switched from left-half to right-half during the 1952–53 season, without inconvenience, as he continued to rack up his tally of appearances. On 27 December 1954, away at Bristol Rovers, he made his 200th League appearance for the club and celebrated with a 4–1 victory. Over the next three months he played in all six of County's FA Cup matches as they advanced to the sixth round, before losing to York City at Meadow Lane in front of a ground record attendance of 47,310 people.

The following season would be Harry's last with the Magpies and he bowed out on 10 March 1956 after a home defeat to Hull City. After leaving Notts County, Harry spent a couple of seasons playing non-League football. He later worked for the *Nottingham Evening Post* but returned to Scotland after retirement. Harry died in Kilmarnock in 1997, aged 72.

Sam Allardyce

Date of birth: 19 October 1954, Dudley

Notts County record:

Manager: 1997–1999

Played for: Bolton Wanderers, Sunderland, Millwall, Coventry City, Huddersfield Town, Preston North End, West Bromwich Albion, Tampa Bay (USA)

Also managed: Limerick, Blackpool, Bolton Wanderers

Sam Allardyce's reign as Notts County manager was fairly brief and ended controversially but his reign will not be easily forgotten.

As a player Sam had played for a number of teams, but he will best be remembered as a 'no-nonsense' centre-half who did not believe in taking prisoners. His best years were undoubtedly spent with Bolton Wanderers, with whom he made his League debut in 1973, coincidentally in a 3–1 home defeat to Notts County. It was with Bolton that he won a Second Division championship medal in 1978 but he endeared himself at all of his other clubs for his thorough professionalism and whole-hearted commitment.

Moving into the coaching side of the game, Sam spent time on the backroom staff at both Preston and Sunderland before landing his first managerial position in the Republic of Ireland with Limerick. He was soon offered his first Football League appointment with Blackpool and led the Seasiders from the foot of the table in 1994 into play-off contenders two years later. Missing out on promotion proved to be costly, as Sam reflected later. 'I must be the only manager to have been sacked by somebody in prison. The chairman was inside and we'd lost in the play-off semi-final to Bradford City. After a board meeting I thought everything was OK but he sent a message from his cell saying that I should be sacked!'

Sam's work had been noticed and Derek Pavis moved swiftly to secure his services at Meadow Lane. 'I felt harshly treated by Blackpool but at least it meant that I ended up at Notts County, so it can't all have been bad.'

County were already sliding towards relegation and Allardyce's appointment came too late to halt the slide. Nevertheless, his quest for an immediate return to the Second Division was spectacularly successful. The 1997–98 season was the stuff of dreams for Magpies supporters. Record after record tumbled as Notts clinched the title before the end of March. A run of 10 consecutive League wins ensured that Sam's team would enter the history books as one of the club's most successful ever.

Hopes were high of even more success but they were dashed when Sam handed in his notice in October 1999. The fans were stunned and the County board was not happy when he was unveiled as the new manager of Bolton just five days later. The matter went to a tribunal and it was clear that no one was happy in the manner in which his switch of clubs had happened so quickly.

Despite Notts County's disappointment at losing Sam, no one can deny that he has transformed his old club in spectacular fashion. He led them into the Premiership in just his second season there and confounded the critics by becoming even more successful. During the 2003–04 season, the Trotters reached the League Cup final at the Millennium Stadium, where they were defeated by Middlesbrough. The following year a sixth-place finish in the League ensured that European football would arrive at the Reebok Stadium during 2005–06, with a confirmed place in the UEFA Cup.

While his stock is undoubtedly still rising, 'Big Sam' still regards himself as being one of the unfashionable managers. 'The big clubs are looking to attract overseas managers now', he says. 'Not because they are better managers or coaches but because of their knowledge of other countries and overseas players. I won't get one of these jobs unless I change my name to Sam Allardici!'

In March 2005, 'Big Sam' returned to Meadow Lane to attend a Notts County Supporters Trust fundraising evening. The former Magpies manager revealed that he had driven past Meadow Lane many times since leaving, without going inside. Should he have been in any doubt as to the reception that he would receive then he had not reckoned upon the Magpies supporters, who gave him a standing ovation.

Larger than life, and always with a quip, Sam was deadly serious when he admitted, 'Nothing has been more special to me than winning that championship [with Notts County] and the manner in which we achieved it.'

Bill Ashurst

Date of birth: 4 May 1894, Willington, County Durham
Died: 26 January 1947

Notts County record:
Appearances: League 200, FA Cup 22
Goals: League 0, FA Cup 0
Debut: 28 August 1920 v Bristol City (a) won 1–0

Also played for: Leeds City, Newark Town, Lincoln City, West Bromwich Albion, England (5 caps)

Bill Ashurst was a wonderfully consistent right-back who made the Notts number two jersey his own during the 1920s. During that period he had few equals in the position and he was selected to play for England on five occasions.

He joined Notts from Lincoln City, having been originally at Leeds City, a side wound up for financial irregularities. Like the rest of his Leeds teammates, Bill's future was in the hands of the highest bidder. Like some barbaric livestock auction, players were paraded on 17 October 1919 at The Metropole Hotel in Leeds. Bill's new employers bid £500 for his services. At the same auction Notts successfully bid £1,000 for striker Billy McLeod.

Bill's stay at Lincoln was brief and he joined the Meadow Lane staff in time for the 1920–21 season. With Bill on the right-hand side of the defence and Horace Cope on the left, Notts boasted one of the most reliable full-back pairings in the land. As the laws of the game stood at that time, the offside trap involved three players, rather than the two of the modern era. Ashurst and Cope perfected it to a fine art to frustrate opposition forwards.

It was extremely rare for either to be absent, with only the occasional injury ruling out either. Consequently, although it was never pretty to watch, Notts were usually fairly solid at the back.

The Magpies enjoyed some high-profile FA Cup encounters around the time of Bill joining them. His first match in the competition, against Aston Villa, was witnessed by a then ground record of 45,014. After a goalless draw the replay was lost at Villa Park, but the experience stood Notts in good stead. The following season saw the Second Division side progress to the semi-final for the first time since they had won the cup in 1894. Ten matches were needed to reach the last four but the fairytale ended at Turf Moor, Burnley, with a 3–1 loss to Huddersfield Town.

By now, Bill had established himself as a permanent fixture in the Notts line-up and he only missed one match during the 1922–23 season, a key factor in the side winning the Second Division title and promotion to the top flight. Notts kept 13 clean sheets in the first 21 games and only conceded one goal in the other eight matches, until a 2–1 defeat at Fulham on Boxing Day – just 24 hours after the two sides had met in Nottingham.

Bill joined his teammates in collecting his championship medal and then had additional cause for celebration with the news that he had been selected for England's end-of-season tour to Sweden. On 21 May 1923 he made his international debut in Stockholm, and lined up against the same opposition three days later, with England winning both matches. Notts established themselves as a mid-table First Division side and Bill picked up three more international caps, playing against Scotland, Wales and Belgium.

The full-back's consistency was revered throughout the land but the 1925–26 season was full of frustration for club and individual alike. The offside law was amended to something resembling the modern version, but Notts were slow to grasp the implications. Opponents helped themselves to preventable goals as the water-tight defence of recent seasons began to spring leaks.

Injuries took their toll on both full-backs, virtually for the first time in their careers, and relegation was the outcome. Ashurst missed 23 League games in all, including the final 18, before it was confirmed that he needed a cartilage operation. He returned, fully fit, for the start of the new campaign and played in the opening 16 games but Bill's stay at Meadow Lane ended in November 1926 when he moved back to the First Division with a transfer to West Bromwich Albion for a fee of around £3,000.

In his six-year stay at Meadow Lane, Bill Ashurst played in exactly 200 League matches for Notts.

Jeff Astle

Date of birth: 13 May 1942, Eastwood, Notts
Died: 19 January 2002

Notts County record:
Appearances: League 103, FA Cup 5, League Cup 8
Goals: League 31, FA Cup 1, League Cup 9
Debut: 23 September 1961 v Reading (a) lost 2–4

Also played for: West Bromwich Albion, Dunstable, Weymouth, England (5 caps)

Notts County have had their fair share of quality strikers over the years and nothing pleases the fans more than a home-grown success. Local lad Jeff Astle had played briefly for the John Player side, before being taken on the Notts staff, and was still only 19 when he was introduced into their first team.

Supporter David Richmond recalls his friendship with Jeff. 'We were both Eastwood boys and both attended the Devonshire Drive School. We walked to and from school together and Jeff would always be talking about football. When Notts signed him from John Player he was so excited.'

He made just seven appearances that first season without getting on the scoresheet, but his season did end on a high when he grabbed the winning goal against Nottingham Forest in the County Cup final. The following season, in 1962–63, Jeff really came to the fore. Playing alongside Tony Hateley he demonstrated an eye for goal that would serve him well throughout his career. The pair scored 41 goals between them, although Notts could do no better than a seventh-place finish.

Jeff's only Notts hat-trick came at home against Oldham Athletic but his all-round play was also drawing admiring glances and it was inevitable that his talents would be displayed at a higher level. In September 1964 a bid of £22,500 from West Brom was accepted, so Jeff swapped the Magpies' famous colours for the stripes of the Albion.

The record books reveal that Jeff went on to win only five caps for England – a relatively modest return. What they do not convey is that for much of the period when he was at his peak, the national side were enjoying their reign as World Champions and the men who had participated in that success were not going to be displaced easily. Additionally, substitutes were a fairly recent innovation and managers, especially at international level, did not make wholesale changes as they do in the modern game. So Jeff's caps were fully deserved and earned on merit.

Successful as he had been at Meadow Lane, no one could argue that he became an even bigger sensation following his transfer. The Baggies fans still refer to him as 'The King' and it is understandable to see why he is so revered. In 361 matches for them, he scored a staggering 174 times. Jeff's goals helped take the side to four domestic finals in as many years. He twice scored in League Cup finals, against West Ham United in 1966 and against Manchester City four years later.

His most memorable, most important goal came in 1968 at Wembley Stadium. The FA Cup final against Everton had remained scoreless and entered extra time. Two minutes in and the Albion mounted an attack. Jeff rode a challenge from Howard Kendall and tried his luck with his right foot. The ball was instantly blocked and rebounded to the striker. This time it was on his left and a first-time drive arrowed into the net, beyond the dive of Gordon West, the Everton goalkeeper. It was to be the winning goal – the score by which Jeff would be identified for all time and, with it, he became the first player to score in each round of a season's competition.

Brief though it was, Jeff's international career was not without incident. His debut came at Wembley in a 2–1 win over Wales in 1969. A tour of Mexico followed, with England playing two matches against their hosts – one of them was deemed an 'unofficial international'. Jeff scored twice in that game in a 4–0 win. Sadly, they would be the only goals he would register in an England jersey, though he would return to the same Guadalajara Stadium one year later to participate in a much more important encounter.

The defending World Champions were trailing Brazil 1–0 in a group game of the 1970 World Cup Finals when Jeff was introduced as a 64th minute substitute, replacing Francis Lee. Ten minutes from time a glorious opportunity was squandered when he ballooned a close-range chance high over the bar. His look of disbelief was mirrored by the millions of television viewers. Four days later Jeff played in the 1–0 win against Czechoslovakia, not realising that would be his last outing for England.

Injuries began to take their toll and he dramatically bowed out of top-flight football by leaving The Hawthorns to play for Barry Fry at Dunstable. This did not last long and the former England international was soon shining in a different sphere – having set up his own window-cleaning business.

In 1995, Jeff emerged from the wilderness by becoming a regular 'guest singer' on the *Fantasy Football* show, hosted by Baggies fan Frank Skinner and David Baddiel.

Tragically, in 2002, Jeff collapsed at his daughter's home and died, aged just 59. Over 700 mourners turned up to pay their respects at his funeral. David Richmond reflects the thoughts of them all, 'He was a great player and a true gentleman.'

Raddy Avramovic

Date of birth: 29 November 1949, Croatia

Notts County record:
Appearances: League 149, FA Cup 3, League Cup 14, Others 15
Debut: 18 August 1979 v Cardiff City (h) won 4–1

Also played for: NK Rijeka (Yugoslavia), Coventry City, Inter Montreal, Yugoslavia (3 caps)

Coach/Manager: Sur FC (Oman), Oman National Team, Kuwait Olympic Team, Kuwait National Team, Ruwi FC (Oman), Singapore National Team

Towards the latter part of the 1970s the influx of continental stars into the domestic game even reached Meadow Lane. Notts' scouting network was active and their homework reaped dividends when Jimmy Sirrel was suitably impressed to splash out a then club record fee of £200,000 to sign 29-year-old Radojko Avramovic from Yugoslav side NK Rijeka.

Raddy had just earned international recognition, so it seemed slightly illogical for the big goalkeeper to contemplate a move to the East Midlands. 'With Rijeka I'd won the Yugoslav Cup for two consecutive seasons', he says. 'I'd always wanted to play in England as I felt it was the best League in the world. Moving to Notts County gave me the fresh challenge I was looking for.'

Adapting to unfamiliar conditions and struggling with a new language tested Raddy's resolve to the limit but the goalkeeper quickly made friends and began to show why he had gained such a glowing reputation. A player who had recently moved away from Meadow Lane was particularly helpful to the new recruit, together with his wife Bratislava and their son, Ivan. 'Everyone at Notts County was so kind towards me and my family. We lived near to Steve Carter and his wife Marie. They really helped us settle and I'll always be grateful to them for their kindness.'

For four seasons Raddy maintained a high level of consistency and more than played his part as Notts returned to the top flight of the English game. 'If I had to pick one day out, above all others, it would have to be the win at Chelsea which secured our promotion to Division One after 55 years. It was what we had worked so hard to achieve and it clearly meant so much to so many people.'

Critics often say that imported players do not fully understand the importance of local derbies – Raddy is one of the exceptions. 'We all really enjoyed the 2–0 away win over Nottingham Forest in 1982. I desperately wanted to keep a clean sheet that day and was delighted to save a penalty from John Robertson.'

Raddy was an ever-present that season but another of his proudest memories from his days at Meadow Lane came at the end of the 1982–83 season when he was presented with the supporters' Player of the Year award. That summer he said his goodbyes to the County fans and moved to Coventry City for a short spell. Raddy, though, was already working hard for the next phase of his career. 'I passed all my coaching badges during my time in England and returned to Yugoslavia to assist a few clubs. Then I got the chance to move to Oman in 1991, where I helped Sur FC to promotion in my first season and then we won the cup final the year after.'

Raddy's early success had clearly impressed. He was appointed National Team Coach to begin an amazing period of coaching at the highest level. He took Kuwait to the Sydney Olympics in 2000 before succeeding the Scotland-bound Berti Vogts as National Coach.

His stock was high as he inspired his Kuwait side to the quarter-finals of the Asian Games. A return to League management brought a domestic title in Oman with Ruwi, which heralded another National Team appointment with Singapore, whom he led during the 2006 World Cup qualifiers.

With more than 35 years involvement in the game, Raddy still recalls his days with Notts County as amongst his favourite. 'The atmosphere at the club was something special. The bond amongst the players, the coaching staff and the supporters was so close and friendly. I look back and think of us all being one big, happy family.'

Ian Baraclough

Date of birth: 4 December 1970, Leicester

Notts County record:

Appearances: League 212, FA Cup 15, League Cup 12, Others 6
Goals: League 15, FA Cup 0, League Cup 1, Others 0
Debut: 14 October 1995 v Rotherham United (h) won 2–1

Also played for: Leicester City, Wigan Athletic, Grimsby Town, Lincoln City, Mansfield Town, Queens Park Rangers, Scunthorpe United

Ian Baraclough was almost three players in one during his time with Notts County. More than comfortable at left-back, in centre midfield or out on the left flank, he clocked up over 200 appearances for the Magpies during two separate spells at Meadow Lane.

He began his footballing career as a trainee at his home-town club, Leicester City, but was given his first taste of League football during loan spells at Wigan Athletic and Grimsby Town. His move to the Mariners became a permanent deal but it was not until he had moved to Lincoln City in August 1992 that Ian's career began to take off. Impressive performances during 91 League and cup outings for the Imps attracted the attentions of Mansfield Town, who became his next employers in 1994.

'Bara' joined Notts for the first time on 13 October 1995 when a fee of £150,000 secured his services. His introduction to the Magpies line-up coincided with the team hitting a purple patch and winning five out of six matches to move into the top three in the table.

Included in those victories was a pulsating 4–3 win at Burnley, with Ian scoring his first goal for County. The regular season ended with the disappointment of a fourth-placed finish, tempered by a place in the play-offs. Unlike the two previous occasions that Notts reached the final at Wembley, this time there was no happy ending with the Magpies losing 2–0 to Bradford City.

Strong and determined in the tackle and decent in the air, Ian came to Notts with an additional string to his bow. As a dead-ball taker he was accurate and effective. Free-kicks and corners became entrusted to his magical left foot, often with devastating effect.

There was even more dejection for County followers at the end of the 1996–97 campaign, with the club relegated to the fourth tier of the domestic game. The arrival of Sam Allardyce as boss rejuvenated the Magpies' fortunes as they made sure of promotion at the first time of asking.

In March 1998, with 'Big Sam's' side riding high at the top of the table, Notts were prepared to allow Ian to join Queens Park Rangers. During his time with the Hoops, he played in 125 League matches, many of them as skipper. Things went well for Ian at Loftus Road until his club were beset by crippling financial problems. Desperate to reduce the wage bill, several players were allowed to leave. Ian was amongst them, returning to Meadow Lane on a free transfer.

His second County debut came in a 4–2 defeat at Port Vale in August 2001. It turned out to be a depressing season for the club. Despite a change of manager, with Billy Dearden replacing Gary Brazil, there were genuine fears of relegation until a last-day victory confirmed safety.

In September 2002, Ian ruptured his ankle ligaments in a match against Luton Town and was forced to miss two months of the season. Meanwhile, the off-field situation at Notts was becoming increasingly difficult for all concerned, including the players, and there were genuine fears that the club might fold. Administrators were brought in and the future appeared bleak. For Ian this was an unwelcome case of lightning striking twice after similar problems had beset his previous club.

The 2003–04 campaign was all about survival and, although Notts again succumbed to relegation, they managed to preserve their Football League status. Amid a plethora of well-wishers and fundraising activities came a welcome spot of good fortune as Notts were paired away at Chelsea in the League Cup. A paying gate of over 35,000 ensured a hefty cheque would find its way back to Meadow Lane. For Ian and the rest of his teammates the match provided an opportunity to compete against some of the Premiership's finest and they acquitted themselves admirably before going down by four goals to two.

Towards the end of that campaign Ian was informed that he was not being retained. Nevertheless, he was included for the final match of the season at home to Oldham Athletic – his 200th League start for Notts.

Ian joined Scunthorpe United in time for the start of the 2004–05 season. Proving that there was still plenty of life left in the legs, he turned in a hugely consistent season, missing just one match, as The Iron clinched promotion to Division One.

Brian Bates

Date of birth: 4 December 1944, Beeston, Notts

Notts County record:

Appearances: League 128, FA Cup 2, League Cup 7
Goals: League 24, FA Cup 0, League Cup 1
Debut: 18 April 1964 v Bristol Rovers (a) lost 0–4

Also played for: Mansfield Town, Boston United, Ilkeston Town, Atherstone Town, Tamworth

Winger Brian Bates was one of the last amateur players to represent the Magpies. Between 1963 and 1966 he played for County while still at teacher training college.

'There was quite a bit of controversy about it', recalls Brian. 'The college football team wanted me to play for them and the situation actually made the national press. There was a fellow called Johnny Barr at college with me and he kept goal for Barnet. They enjoyed a good run in the FA Cup and he was forced to choose between playing for them or continuing his studies. Johnny quit and went off to play football.'

Although Brian continued with his education he did manage to break into the County team. 'I was given my debut at the end of the 1963–64 season. The club had already been relegated and we went to Bristol Rovers and got hammered. I later learned that the manager, Eddie Lowe, hadn't been that keen to include me as an amateur but he hadn't anything to lose as we were already down. Despite the result it was pleasing to have played in the first team.'

The following term he made just five starts but had the satisfaction of scoring his first League goal. 'It was away at Halifax. I just ran on to a through ball and banged it in from the edge of the box. It was a great feeling to actually score a League goal.'

With Tim Coleman now in charge, the 1965–66 season was Brian's breakthrough year but it started in somewhat bizarre fashion. 'I hadn't been involved on the opening day of the season and it was still the college summer break, so I'd got a job working for Tooley and Sons Wholesaler's on the fruit and veg market. I'd got up at about 5.30, worked from 6.00 'til 9.30 then gone training. Afterwards the manager told me he wanted me to travel to Stockport that night with the first team. I went, played and scored two decent goals. From then on I felt I was accepted as one of the players.'

Brian enjoyed a marvellous season but ended it with an injury. 'I chipped a bone in my left ankle and had to rest up for a while. I didn't even go to the end of season dinner, where they announced I was the Player of the Year. It was that good a secret they didn't even think to invite the winner!'

During the close season one or two clubs enquired about Brian's availability. 'I'd played against West Ham for the college and run their full-back, John Bond, dizzy. Ron Greenwood had told me to keep in touch and there were offers from Preston and Sheffield United but I was happy to stay at Notts and accept their offer to become a professional.'

After making more than 100 League appearances for the Magpies, Brian moved on to Mansfield Town but the move quickly turned sour. 'I played in a League Cup-tie against Notts County and scored against my good friend Mick Rose but then got another ankle injury. This time I'd also done ligament damage. Nowadays the treatment would have been much better but it was still fairly primitive then and the injury didn't respond. It effectively ended my career although I was able to stay in the game, playing non-League.'

The decision to qualify as a teacher stood Brian in good stead as he had an alternative career to fall back on but he also turned to coaching and had a brief spell in charge of County's youth team.

Brian is actively involved as a member of the Ex-Notts County Players Association and remains a regular and popular visitor to Meadow Lane.

Tristan Benjamin

Date of birth: 1 April 1957, St Kitts, West Indies

Notts County record:

Appearances: League 311, FA Cup 17, League Cup 29, Others 28

Goals: League 4, FA Cup 0, League Cup 0, Others 1

Debut: 2 April 1975 v West Bromwich Albion (a) lost 1–4

Also played for: Chesterfield, Corby Town

A casual glance at any Magpies team line-up, photographed between the mid-1970s and the early 1980s, will readily fall upon the unmistakable presence of Tristan Benjamin. Sporting one of the liveliest Afros you could ever wish to see, the talented defender shone for County for over a decade.

'Benjy' was born in the West Indies but moved to Nottingham, with his family, as a youngster. Graduating through County's youth sides he was handed the perfect birthday present by manager Jimmy Sirrel. A day after his 18th he was selected to make his first-team debut away at West Bromwich Albion.

Over the next three or so seasons he had to bide his time, waiting patiently for a lengthy run in the side. His five appearances, four of them as a substitute, during the 1975–76 season yielded two goals – a false dawn as it turned out in terms of 'Tristan the goalscorer' – he only added another three more in the next 350-plus matches.

'Utility player' is an almost derisory phrase in footballing terms but occasionally a player comes along to whom it is meant as a sincere compliment. Benjy was such a player. His own qualities, plus the needs of the team, dictated that Tristan was constantly moved from position to position until 1980, when Pedro Richards switched to a new role as sweeper.

Although he had played at right-back many times before, his game simply flourished when he was given the number two jersey on a permanent basis. Softly spoken, in comparison to many of his colleagues, Tristan was always prepared to let his football do the talking. His consistency was to be admired as he played in every single League match of the successful 1980–81 promotion season. As much as anyone else, he enjoyed the celebrations as the fans rejoiced at Stamford Bridge after County's elevation to the top flight had been assured.

If anyone felt the step up in class might be too big a gulf for Benjy to overcome, they were soon mistaken. Up against the country's best wide players, he rarely, if ever, came out second best. A few calls for international recognition went unheeded but his reputation had been firmly established.

During Notts' three seasons in the old First Division, Tristan played in 90 matches, maintaining excellent form throughout. The club, though, were on the slide and successive relegations found them back in the third tier by 1985–86. Reverting to a midfield berth, Tristan made 43 appearances that season to earn the supporters' Player of the Year award.

The following campaign was to be Benjy's last as a Magpie. A 1–1 draw at Newport County on 1 November 1986 brought up the milestone of his 300th League appearance for the club but he only featured 11 more times before bringing the curtain down on his days at Meadow Lane. His career was extended with a move to Chesterfield before he left the game altogether to begin life as a social worker.

The Afro may have long gone but Tristan's service to Notts County will never be forgotten.

Tony Bircumshaw

Date of birth: 8 February 1945, Mansfield

Notts County record:

Appearances: League 148, FA Cup 6, League Cup 11

Goals: League 1, FA Cup 0, League Cup 0

Debut: 3 April 1961 v Brentford (a) lost 0–3

Also played for: Hartlepool United, Nuneaton Borough

They say 'give youth a chance' and manager Frank Hill certainly adhered to the old maxim. Tony Bircumshaw was aged just 16 years and 54 days when he made his bow in the Notts County first team.

'I'd left school the previous Easter and graduated from the third team into the reserve side', says Tony. 'Arthur Dixon was the club's physio at the time and he also ran the reserves. He kept telling me to continue playing as I was and maybe I'd get a chance in the first team.'

That chance soon came around. 'I was called into the manager's office and told I was playing the next day at Brentford. I didn't know what to say – I was flabbergasted. Mr Hill said he was going to have a look at me for two matches and however well I'd done I would still be rested after that. He was true to his word – we lost at Brentford but then I played in the next home game. I didn't really know if I was coming or going to start with but soon settled into the matches and really enjoyed them.'

The young full-back did not have to look far for a friendly face, as brother Peter was playing ahead of him on the left wing. 'Some people say it must have been awkward having your brother in the same side but it was never a problem for us. He was a good player – very quick and capable of scoring 20 goals a season. For a while we had two pairs of brothers in the same team as Peter and John Butler were also included on occasions.'

Tony went on to make 165 first-team appearances for Notts, scoring just once. Not surprisingly, he remembers the goal clearly. 'It was away against Brighton and I'd been hurt. I tackled the winger and somehow slipped underneath him – he came down with all his weight on my knee. It swelled up and felt like it was going to explode but we didn't have substitutes in those days.'

For the remainder of the match Tony became a passenger, playing out on the wing, but he was able to limp forward for a corner. 'The ball came across but everyone missed it. It came out to me at the edge of the box, I struck it right-footed – and it flew in!'

Comfortable on either side of the defence, Tony eventually left Notts to join Hartlepool United and later Nuneaton Borough – managed at the time by old schoolboy chum, David Pleat.

After finishing his playing career the former Magpie worked in insurance, graduating to Branch Manager. Now retired, Tony lives in the Mansfield area, close enough to keep an eye on the fortunes of his old side – and monitor his record of being the club's youngest-ever League player.

A 'new kid on the block' looked likely to lower the age limit in January 1999. 'Jermaine Pennant was even younger than me when he played in an FA Cup-tie and great things were expected of him but he moved on to Arsenal before he had the chance to play in the League side. It seems he's let himself down on occasions – I just hope he manages to turn his career around. I imagine one day someone will come along who's even younger than I was – until then it's quite nice to see my name still there in the record books.'

Charley Bisby

Date of birth: 10 September 1904, Mexborough, Yorkshire

Died: June 1977

Notts County record:

Appearances: League 206, FA Cup 9

Goals: League 1, FA Cup 0

Debut: 16 October 1926 v Reading (a) lost 1–7

Also played for: Denaby United, Coventry City, Mansfield Town, Peterborough United

Clarence Charles Bisby was still only 21 when he joined Notts County in the summer of 1926. Over the next six seasons he developed into one of the most consistent left-backs in the land and compiled over 200 League appearances for the Magpies.

Known to one and all as 'Charley', the youngster was soon seen as the heir apparent to Horace Cope, who had worn the number three jersey with such distinction for a number of years. His League debut was memorable for all the wrong reasons as Notts were thumped 1–7 at Reading but it was evident that the solidly built defender was a whole-hearted competitor who rarely shirked a challenge.

He made 28 appearances in his first season at Meadow Lane and his consistency saw him through an ever-present campaign the following year. The highlight of that season was an incredible 9–0 home victory over Barnsley.

The 1928–29 programme began in emphatic fashion for the Magpies. For the first 10 League matches the side remained unchanged but, despite winning seven of those matches, a disappointing fifth place was the best that County could muster. Nevertheless, the season did produce one defining moment in Charley's career. Prioritising his defensive duties above everything else, the full-back rarely ventured too far into opposition territory but he did get close enough to score his only Notts goal in a 3–0 home victory over Wolves on 1 April 1929.

The Magpies suffered relegation at the end of the following season but they were able to bounce back at the first time of asking, with Charley shining as brightly as the Third Division South championship medal he would always cherish.

As a complete defensive unit, Notts had been magnificent, conceding only 13 goals at home all season. The title was won in convincing style and the impetus was carried over into the new season. The 1931–32 season was to be Charley's last at Meadow Lane but he achieved the outstanding milestone of 200 League appearances for the club towards the end of the campaign.

During the close season he signed for Coventry City but life at Highfield Road got off to a frustrating start when he sustained a knee injury and had to have a cartilage removed. Upon recovery he went on to be appointed as club captain and enjoyed a second Division Three South championship success in the 1935–36 season.

After notching up more than 100 first-team appearances for the Sky Blues, Charley moved on again, spending brief spells at Mansfield Town and Peterborough United. The outbreak of World War Two effectively ended Charley's playing career and he was called up to join the Army. However, most of the next few years were spent as a prisoner of war after the invasion of Crete.

After the war Charley worked for Coventry City as a scout before returning to Nottingham, with employment as a stock controller for the Corona soft drinks company. He was regarded as a hero at Corona when, in 1971, a fire was ablaze at the factory and Charley bravely drove 14 vans to safety from an adjoining building.

Charley Bisby passed away in 1977, aged 72, but the fortunes of his former club are now closely followed from afar. Grandson Bruce Stevens lives in Kelowna BC, after Charley's daughter married and moved to Canada in 1946. 'Sadly, I never did get to meet him as he died shortly before I visited Nottingham. My great uncle Eric Massey still lives in Derby and tells me what a popular guy Charley was. I still look for County's results and hope to get the chance to visit and see them in 2006.'

Les Bradd

Date of birth: 5 November 1947, Buxton, Derbyshire

Notts County record:

Appearances: League 394, FA Cup 22, League Cup 17, Others 8

Goals: League 125, FA Cup 4, League Cup 7, Others 1

Debut: 4 October 1967 v Crewe Alexandra (h) won 1–0

Also played for: Rotherham United, Stockport County, Wigan Athletic, Bristol Rovers, Kettering Town

No other Notts County player has scored more goals in the Football League than Les Bradd. With 125 strikes for the club, he stands 16 clear of his closest rival, former teammate Tony Hateley.

During most of his time with the Magpies, Les played as the main target-man but he admits he enjoyed a different role during the brief period he played alongside Hateley. 'My most successful season, in terms of goals scored, was when I played just off Tony, profiting from his knock-downs and flick-ons.' That season, 1971–72, resulted in 21 goals for the man nicknamed 'Bomber' by fans and teammates. Not surprisingly, his achievements earned him the club's Player of the Year award.

Despite all his achievements in the game as a proven goalscorer, Les feels that signing as a full-time professional remains his proudest moment. 'Like most youngsters I always wanted to be a footballer but couldn't ever see it happening. I didn't even get invited for trials with Buxton, my local non-League team!'

Les was lost to football for a couple of years. 'I began working as an apprentice fitter and welder in a limestone quarry and couldn't get Saturday afternoons off. At 17 I got the chance to play again, for a village team called Earl Sterndale. After one match a guy approached me and asked if I'd be interested in going for a trial with Rotherham United.' The young striker impressed sufficiently and was handed a debut by the Millers for a match at Aston Villa in 1967. He made just a handful of appearances for the South Yorkshire side but got on the scoresheet on his first appearance at Meadow Lane – against Notts. 'Dave Watson marked me that night but I managed to score the only goal in a 1–0 League Cup win.'

Shortly afterwards Les was informed that County had bid £1,000 for his services and it was felt that he ought to accept the opportunity. Billy Gray was the Magpies manager at the time and Les pays tribute to his first County boss. 'Billy's role in the club's subsequent rise up the divisions is often forgotten. He began to put together a decent squad, which was then handed on to Jack Wheeler and then Jimmy Sirrel.'

It was under Sirrel's guidance that Notts eventually ended their seven-year exile in the Fourth Division. 'Jimmy made us more professional. Every day we would play a full-scale practice match and he developed a winning mentality into us all. All of the players had nothing but the greatest of respect for the man.'

Les contributed 13 League and cup goals in the 1972–73 season, helping the club to their second promotion in three years.

Curiously, although it is through his League goals tally that Les remains in the County record books, some of his finest moments came in the League Cup competition. 'I usually seemed to do well in that competition', he reflects. 'One of my best goals for the club came against Stoke City. Over the years we had some really good results - I managed to score both goals when we knocked Everton out and no one will ever forget the night we went to Elland Road and beat Leeds United.'

On 17 April 1976, 'Bomber' scored his 100th League goal for Notts during a comfortable 4–0 victory over Fulham. He added a further 25 before moving on to join Stockport County during the summer of 1978. Les gave the Magpies more than a decade of loyal service as a player and returned at the end of his career to raise money for the club as a sales executive for County 75 Lottery team.

In 1994 he moved across the Trent to join Nottingham Forest's backroom staff, initially as assistant Commercial Manager and latterly as Corporate Sales Manager.

Gordon Bradley

Date of birth: 20 May 1925, Scunthorpe

Notts County record:

Appearances: League 192, FA Cup 10
Goals: League 1
Debut: 9 September 1950 v Grimsby Town (a) won 4-1

Also played for: Leicester City, Cambridge City, Glentoran

In an era when goalkeepers were not as protected as they are these days, Notts County possessed one of the bravest and most reliable in Gordon Bradley. Many felt that his performances should have been rewarded with an international call-up and later it emerged that he had come close, as Gordon's son, David, later discovered. 'Apparently he'd been considered for an England tour of Sweden but the selectors changed their minds because they felt he seldom looked as if he was trying!'

Gordon certainly was trying – in fact he never gave anything less than 100 percent – but his composure and reassuring presence was often mistaken for someone not giving their all. Aside from his many other qualities, Gordon was a wonderful catcher of a football. Many of his contemporaries began to favour the punch as a means of clearing their lines but the Meadow Lane favourite preferred the more conventional method of goalkeeping. There were no fancy gloves then – just bare hands or woollen ones in the wet!

Gordon joined Notts in 1950 after eight years on the books of Leicester City, for whom he had played in the 1949 FA Cup final at Wembley Stadium against Wolves. During his first couple of seasons at Meadow Lane he shared the goalkeeping duties with Roy Smith but from early 1952 until 1958 he became first choice.

Reliably consistent, he managed to put together a run of 96 consecutive matches in the League, spanning from 28 March 1953 to 31 August 1955. He had also performed heroics to help County reach the sixth round of the FA Cup.

Possessing a wonderfully safe pair of hands, Gordon always looked immaculate. In the modern game he would have been a sponsor's dream – the handsome, consummate professional with the jet-black hair.

Gordon created a statistical oddity when he returned to Filbert Street to play against his old employers on 22 September 1956. He sustained a hand injury and, in the days before substitutes were allowed, the decision was taken to change goalkeepers and play Gordon out on the wing. Incredibly he got on the scoresheet, heading home a cross from the right. There was no happy ending though, with Leicester City running out 6–3 winners.

Although that was Gordon's only goal in League football, he did build up a bit of a reputation for himself by crashing home penalties in reserve-team matches and friendlies. Indeed, David can recall one such instance. 'I was stood behind the goal at the Meadow Lane end when he scored. He told me afterwards that he'd aimed straight at my face!'

He even embarked upon some friendly banter with an opponent, says David. 'He trotted up the field to take a penalty one day and an opponent told him that he was a terrible goalkeeper, to which my dad replied, 'Maybe – but I can't half take penalties!' Gordon was also the subject of some media humour. 'I remember a cartoon in the Saturday night *Pink Un*, says David. 'It had a goalkeeper in a dungeon getting his already elongated arms pulled on a rack-type affair with something along the lines of "just a few more turns and he'll have as long a reach as Bradley".'

The 1957–58 season was disappointing for all concerned at Meadow Lane. It turned out to be Gordon's last at the club and ultimately finished in relegation. A move to non-Leaguers Cambridge City followed and then the 'keeper moved to Northern Ireland to play for Glentoran.

Gordon was an all-round athlete, excelling at many other sports apart from football. He was a fair table tennis player, winning honours at county level, but his other real love was tennis. He had been good enough to play for Great Britain and competed against some of the best in the world, including the Spanish legend Pancho Gonzalez, who stated afterwards that Gordon was the fittest player he had ever come up against.

In the 1970s, Gordon moved to Bournemouth with wife Noeleen to coach tennis at the West Hants club.

In early 2005 he suffered a stroke and was admitted to Poole General Hospital for a lengthy period of recuperation.

Bill Brindley

Date of birth: 29 January 1947, Nottingham

Notts County record:

Appearances: League 223, FA Cup 12, League Cup 14, Others 1
Goals: League 0, FA Cup 0, League Cup 0, Others 0
Debut: 15 August 1970 v York City (a) drew 0–0

Also played for: Nottingham Forest, Gillingham, Grantham Town, Alfreton Town
Managed: Arnold Town

Bill Brindley has been one of the best-loved characters on the Nottingham football scene for many years. By the end of the 2004–05 season, his involvement with Arnold Town had stretched to more than seven seasons, working with ex-County stars Iain McCulloch and Ray O'Brien, as well as Bryn Gunn, the former 'Forest-er'.

To football fans of a different generation though, Bill will always be remembered as a tough-tackling full-back, blessed with a decent turn of speed and old-fashioned principles. 'I did like to give the winger a whack early on', he admits.

Unable to turn a regular squad place into a consistent spell in the first team, Bill asked to leave Nottingham Forest in the summer of 1970. 'I'd made my mind up after an FA Cup replay away at Carlisle. I'd played against them at home and done well but when I got up there my boots weren't even put out – the manager didn't even have the decency to tell me he was leaving me out.'

Christened 'John' but 'Bill for as long as I can remember', he moved across the Trent in a deal done between the two clubs. 'I learnt later that a couple of other clubs had enquired about me but I wasn't even told. As it happened, joining Notts meant I didn't have to move the family and I knew most of the players anyway.'

Manager Jimmy Sirrel was delighted with his new capture, telling the rest of the squad that he had signed the missing piece of the jigsaw. 'They fell about laughing when I walked in!'

The first season could not have gone any better for the full-back, or his new teammates, as the Division Four championship was lifted. Bill appreciated what it meant to the fans. 'As a local lad I was very aware of how much a little bit of success meant to County's supporters.'

Despite the promotion it was not all 'glitz and glamour' as a lower division footballer. David McVay's excellent book, *Steak Diana Ross*, portrays Bill as a bit of a 'Del Boy' character, with a finger in many pies. 'I suppose it's a fair comment', he says. 'I spent one summer with three jobs, working on the stall at a fruit and veg market, helping out at a greengrocers and running an egg round – I wasn't getting up at four in the morning 'cos I liked it, I had to work because I needed the money.'

Bill was virtually an ever-present over the next four seasons, helping Notts to a second promotion and lifting the Player of the Year award at the end of the 1974–75 season – 'possibly my proudest moment as a footballer'.

A hamstring injury forced the defender to miss almost two months at the start of the next season. The road to recovery was underway when he played in a reserve team match against Doncaster. Incredibly, the next morning, despite stiffness and a few twinges, he was told he had to play again, that night, in a League Cup-tie for the first team. 'The game against Leeds United was massive for us but we had a few injuries. I was nowhere near fit but gave it a go, whacked Eddie Gray a few times and got through it. Pulling off a 1–0 win made it a great night for us all.'

Although Bill scored a goal early in his career for Forest and got another during his days with Gillingham, the record books show a zero against his name from his time with the Magpies. 'I did get one against Bristol Rovers – but it was deflected and given as an own goal. It should have been mine! To be fair I don't know what I was doing across the halfway line – Stubbsy must have carried me up there.'

After a couple of years at Gillingham, Bill returned home to Nottingham where he has enhanced the local non-League scene, played a bit of cricket and regaled friends and acquaintances alike with endless stories of those good old 'Notts County glory days'.

Frank Broome

Date of birth: 11 June 1915, Berkhamsted, Herts
Died: 5 September 1994

Notts County record:
Appearances: League 105, FA Cup 9
Goals: League 35, FA Cup 6
Debut: 29 October 1949 v Walsall (h) drew 1–1

Caretaker manager: January–May 1957
Also played for: Berkhamsted Town, Aston Villa, Derby County, Brentford, Crewe Alexandra, England (7 caps)
Also managed: Exeter City, Southend United

England international Frank Broome came to Meadow Lane late in his career but proved to be a wonderful servant, as player, assistant trainer and caretaker manager.

His eye for goal was evident from an early age. Playing for Berkhamsted Town, his local non-League side, he smashed all sorts of League records by scoring 53 goals during 1933. Football League scouts were alerted and Frank signed for Aston Villa, where his impact on the professional game was instant. His goals helped win a Second Division championship medal in 1938, helping Villa end their long exile outside the top flight.

An England call-up duly arrived, with his debut coinciding with one of the most controversial internationals of all time. With Europe heading for conflict, England travelled to Berlin to meet Germany in front of a crowd of around 120,000. Ill-advisedly, at the request of the British Ambassador, the English players were instructed to perform the 'Nazi salute' during the playing of the German anthem. Although uncomfortable with what they had done, England did not let it affect their performance as they won the match 6–3 – Frank crowning his debut with a goal.

In all, the young striker played for England on seven occasions, scoring three times. During World War Two, Frank 'guested' for Notts County on a number of occasions, as well as turning out for the likes of Birmingham City, Northampton Town, Chesterfield, Nottingham Forest, Watford and Wolves.

Frank moved to Derby County after the war, scoring 45 goals in 112 matches. After three years at the Baseball Ground he joined Notts in a swap deal, which saw goalkeeper Harry Brown move to the Rams.

The 1949–50 season was already proving to be an exciting one for County supporters. Challenging hard for promotion, the arrival of Frank proved to be the missing piece of the puzzle. By now, playing as an orthodox right-winger, Frank was the main supply line for Tommy Lawton. Cross after cross, usually delivered with pinpoint accuracy, set up chances galore for either Lawton to score or to help on for Jackie Sewell to finish.

The local derby with Forest on 3 December 1949 provided Frank with the opportunity to score his first League goal in Notts' colours. His corner had set up Tommy Lawton to bullet home the opening goal and late on the centre-forward returned the favour by teeing up Broome for the second. Although Forest scored a consolation, it was a glorious weekend for Notts fans. There was more joy later in the season, as the double was completed over their near-neighbours on the way to clinching the Division Three South title.

An excellent dead-ball taker, Frank Broome provided many happy memories for 'Pies supporters over the next four years. Frank gained further international recognition in 1951 when he played in two 'unofficial' internationals in Australia, scoring a hat-trick in one of the matches.

He moved to Brentford in 1953 to link up again with Tommy Lawton and had a brief period at Crewe but he came back to Meadow Lane in 1955 as County's assistant trainer. When George Poyser was dismissed in January 1957, Frank was given the manager's job until the end of the season on a caretaker basis.

Lawton came back to take the job full-time but Frank had sampled management and was keen to try his hand at it. He took over as boss of Exeter City for the first of two spells there and also served time as the boss of Southend United.

Frank Broome died in September 1994, aged 79.

Walter Bull

Date of birth: 19 December 1874, Nottingham
Died: 28 July 1952

Notts County record:

Appearances: League 282, FA Cup 18, Others 6
Goals: League 53, FA Cup 5, Others 0
Debut: 3 November 1894 v Woolwich Arsenal (a) lost 1–2

Also played for: St Andrews, Tottenham Hotspur
Managed: Northampton Town

With more than 50 League goals and over 300 first-team appearances for Notts County, Walter Bull is one of the almost-forgotten heroes who gave the club sterling service in their early days.

The local lad was picked up by County from the amateur side St Andrews and was given his debut shortly after the historic 1894 FA Cup win. Jimmy Logan was still around and scored the Notts goal in Walter's debut match, a disappointing defeat, away to Woolwich Arsenal.

In 10 appearances in that first season Walter scored a creditable six goals. A decent return, considering that he played mainly wide on the left, although he was picked for one match at right-back. Highlights of his first few games were a hat-trick at home to Rotherham Town and a goal in the 10–0 thrashing of Burslem Port Vale, the club's record Football League win to that point. Despite not being an out-and-out forward, Walter top scored during the next campaign. He played in all 30 League matches, scoring 15 times, and hit three more goals in the FA Cup competition.

Walter was also an ever-present the following year when Notts achieved promotion by winning the Second Division championship. Amongst his haul of 17 League goals were two more hat-tricks, against Lincoln City and the side he had made his debut against, Woolwich Arsenal – sweet revenge indeed!

Around the turn of the century Walter was converted into an old-fashioned centre-half. Tall and strong, he had the ideal physique to win tackles on the ground and challenges in the air. Critics believed he had few equals in the land in his position, yet amazingly he was overlooked for the full England team. He did make a representative appearance for the Football League side though.

Remaining injury-free, Walter seldom missed a match in almost a decade, thereby compiling a huge tally of appearances for the club. Dropping deeper and deeper, his goals ratio understandably dried up – in the 1903–04 season he did not net a single goal – a stark contrast from his prolific early days.

That was to be his last season with Notts as Tottenham Hotspur splashed out a club record £300 to sign him. For a player in his 30th year it was big money indeed! Walter was equally successful at Spurs, skippering the side in the immediate period before their election to the Football League.

Famously, Walter is credited with playing his part in Arsenal's success. Despite his association with Spurs, he persuaded his good friend Herbert Chapman to become manager at Highbury. Chapman, of course, went on to lead the Gunners to multiple League title successes.

After his own playing days had come to an end Walter briefly entered management himself, with an unspectacular seven-month stint in charge of Northampton Town.

Statistically speaking, Walter Bull was a Notts County giant and fully deserves the accolade of 'legend'.

Dave Calderhead

Date of birth: 19 June 1864, Hurlford, Ayrshire

Died: 9 January 1938

Notts County record:

Appearances: League 278, FA Cup 25, Others 15

Goals: League 12, FA Cup 0, Others 0

Debut: 14 September 1889 v Aston Villa (a) drew 1–1

Also played for: Queen of South Wanderers, Lincoln City, Scotland (1 cap)

Managed: Lincoln City, Chelsea

Modern-day football supporters can easily visualise the moment when the winning captain has climbed the steps to the Royal Box at Wembley and lifted the FA Cup high above his head to acclaim victory. Only one Notts County skipper has ever had the honour bestowed upon him and that was Dave Calderhead, way back in 1894. It is not clear if the Scot actually kissed the trophy but it would have been a particularly sweet moment anyway, as he had played in the final that Notts had lost to Blackburn Rovers three years earlier.

Signing Scottish players was becoming something of a fad when Dave was brought down to join County in 1889, arriving with fellow countrymen Sandy Ferguson, James McMillan, Tom McInnes and the Oswald brothers – the clan 'McMagpie'. Also referred to as David, Davie or Davey, the centre-half had won a cap for Scotland while playing in Dumfries for Queen of the South Wanderers, before travelling south of the border. An excellent distributor of the ball, he was considered tall (5ft 10in) in comparison to many of his contemporaries. He settled in quickly, adapting well to his new surroundings.

Considering that he was later to enjoy FA Cup success with Notts it was somewhat ironic that his first appearance in the competition was tinged with controversy. A third-round tie against Sheffield Wednesday was lost 5–0 on an atrocious pitch. Notts successfully appealed against the quagmire conditions and a replay was ordered. This time Notts won the match but Wednesday claimed that Calderhead and the Oswalds were ineligible to play, having participated in a summer tournament in Scotland. A third match was arranged with Notts forced to leave out the named players and Wednesday won the tie.

The following season Notts reached the final and lost. They also finished third in Division One, making it all the more remarkable that by the time they reached their second final, three years later, they had been relegated. With wins over Burnley (with Calderhead sent off), Burton Wanderers, Nottingham Forest and Blackburn Rovers, Notts reached the 1894 FA Cup final bidding to become the first Division Two side to lift the trophy. Goodison Park was the venue and Bolton Wanderers were overwhelming favourites. But, thanks largely to Jimmy Logan's hat-trick, the Magpies won 4–1. Apart from Dave Calderhead, only two other players appeared in both finals – John Hendry and Alf Shelton.

Despite their cup success it took another three years before promotion was achieved. Dave continued to clock up the appearances for Notts, rarely missing a game, until he signed for Lincoln City in 1899.

Dave's final match for Notts County was away at Preston on 4 November 1899. Tony Brown's excellent book, *Notts County – The Official History 1862–1995* quotes the tribute to Calderhead in the programme notes for that match. 'He retains that excellent judgement for which he is justly famed; feeding his forwards with a master hand (or should we say feet). A well preserved athlete, and an exemplary captain. A steady industrious, gentlemanly player commanding respect of opponents, spectators and committee, he has done as much as anyone to reinstate Notts County in its present highly satisfactory position.'

After his playing days were over Dave turned to management, initially with Lincoln City but then at Chelsea. As boss from 7 September 1907 until 6 May 1933, Dave remains the club's longest-serving manager.

Dave's son, Davie (jnr), followed his father into professional football, playing for Lincoln City, Chelsea, Motherwell, Leicester Fosse, Clapham Orient and then Lincoln City again, as both secretary and manager.

Jimmy Cantrell

Date of birth: 7 May 1882, Chesterfield

Died: 31 July 1960

Notts County record:

Appearances: League 131, FA Cup 5

Goals: League 64, FA Cup 1

Debut: 21 March 1908 v Sheffield United (h) lost 0–3

Also played for: Aston Villa, Tottenham Hotspur, Sutton United

Jimmy Cantrell was one of the most prolific marksmen of his generation. He went on to achieve great success, winning an FA Cup winners' medal with Tottenham Hotspur in 1921.

Before World War One he had spent four very successful seasons with Notts County, rattling in a total of 65 goals from just 136 first-team appearances. He scored a further 78 during wartime 'guest' appearances to lift his Magpies total to a staggering 143 goals.

He had joined the 'Pies from Aston Villa as a willing young centre-forward keen to make his mark in the game. Fleet of foot, and with a striker's eye for a half-chance, Jimmy endeared himself to the supporters as the goals began to accumulate. He twice scored hat-tricks in League matches, both at home. In February 1909, he scored four in the 5–1 thrashing of Manchester City and in October of the same year he scored three against Woolwich Arsenal.

Top scorer in the 1909–10 season, Notts' last one at Trent Bridge, it would have been more than fitting had he scored the club's last goal there. He did not – the honour going to teammate Fred Jones in a 2–3 defeat against Aston Villa, the newly-crowned champions.

That summer Jimmy was a member of the side's first overseas tour, a trip to Denmark. Upon returning, he resumed his place in the side for the first season at Meadow Lane. For the third year in a row he was leading marksman, as the side finished 11th in Division One. His scoring prowess began to attract attention. Although Notts had finished above Tottenham Hotspur during each of the two preceding seasons, the north London club were considered to be progressive and Jimmy was unable to resist an offer to join them in October 1912 for a reported fee of £1,500.

Greater success at Spurs arrived after the war for Jimmy but he was to make a sooner-than-expected return to his old stomping ground. With the outbreak of the conflict he was sent to work at the Ordnance Factory in Nottingham and therefore available to 'guest' for County in their Midlands Section matches. Far from just making up the numbers, Jimmy was a revelation. He top-scored for Notts for four consecutive seasons, banging in a total of 78 goals, 63 of them in League matches. Several times the opposition were really put to the sword, almost single-handedly, by Cantrell. He hit five in an 8-0 win over Grimsby Town, four against Nottingham Forest and three against Derby County, Leicester Fosse and Birmingham.

Hopes were high that he would remain at Meadow Lane but Jimmy returned to White Hart Lane where his goal-scoring exploits continued. In all, he bagged 84 goals in 176 League and cup appearances for the north London side, culminating in that cup-winners medal, at the age of 38, after Wolves had been beaten 1–0 in the final. A total of 72,805 fans crammed into Stamford Bridge to watch that match.

Towards the end of his career, Jimmy joined Sutton Town before once again returning to Nottingham, where he became a licensee.

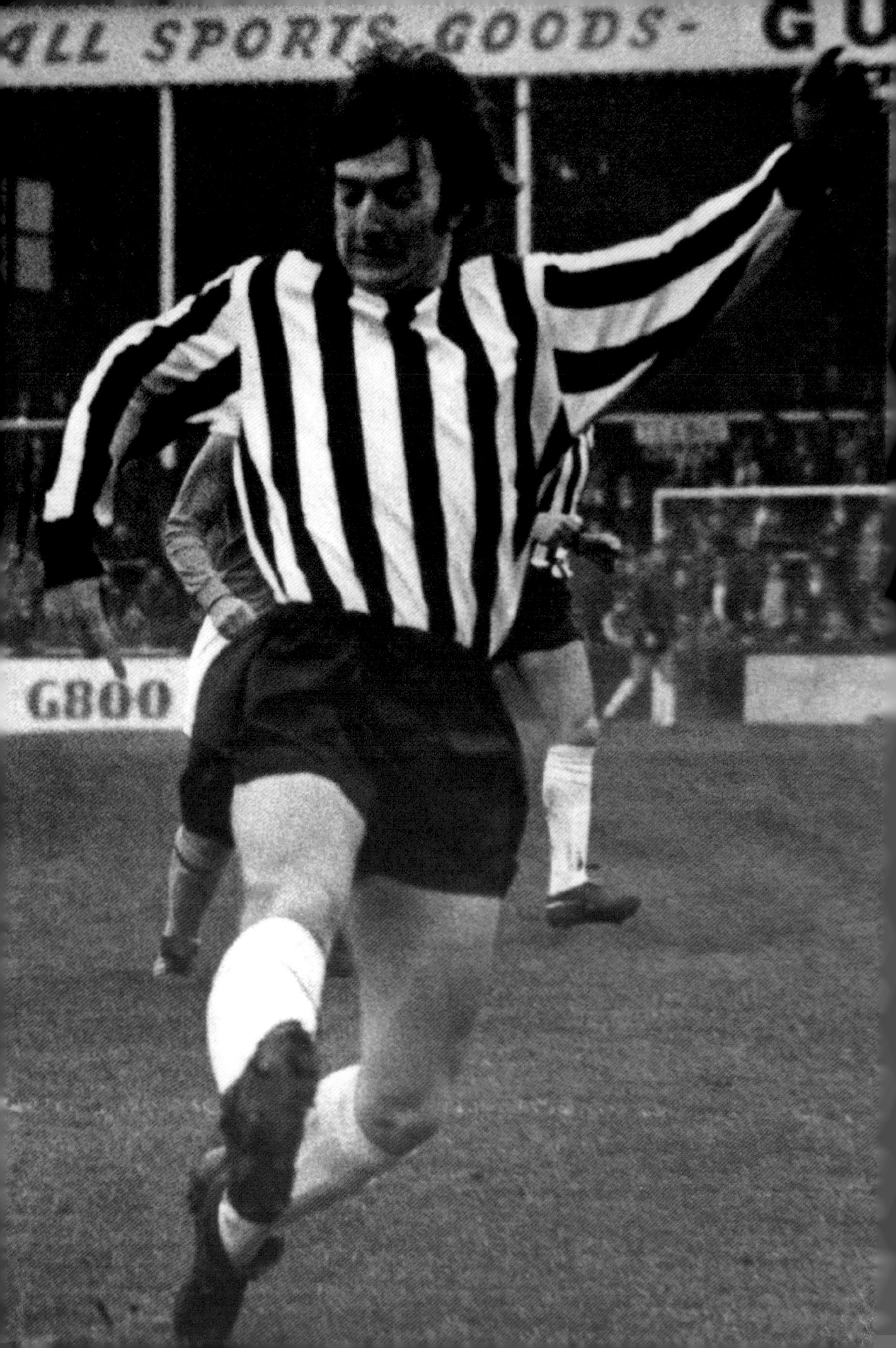
ALL SPORTS GOODS-
GU
G800

Steve Carter

Date of birth: 23 April 1953, Great Yarmouth

Notts County record:

Appearances: League 188, FA Cup 9, League Cup 13, Others 11

Goals: League 21, FA Cup 0, League Cup 3, Others 2

Debut: 12 February 1972 v Oldham Athletic (a) won 1–0

Also played for: Manchester City, Derby County, Bournemouth, Torquay United

It is difficult to assess whether Notts County was a bit of a culture shock for Steve Carter – or vice versa. After signing from Manchester City, the flying winger's flamboyant fashion sense soon earned him the dressing room nickname of 'Flash'.

Steve's new moniker was fairly appropriate for the way he played the game as well. Nippy, with a delightful trick or two, he would twist and turn defenders into a bamboozled submission.

The fans loved him – and so did his teammates. There was often an element of frustration attached though, as the final ball occasionally would not arrive. Tormenting his full-back time and time again was more appealing to Steve than whipping in a first-time cross. His total of assists therefore, would languish way behind the number of occasions when the likes of Les Bradd and Kevin Randall were left unmarked and frustrated in front of goal. Why beat two defenders and cross it if there was a chance of beating three?

Struggling to make inroads into Malcolm Allison's successful Manchester City side, Steve arrived at Meadow Lane on the back of an £18,000 transfer. His debut came in February of the 1971–72 season and between then and the end of the season he made 18 appearances, and chipped in with three goals.

With Jon Nixon being employed on the right flank, Steve hogged the left touchline and the combination served County well as they clinched the runners-up spot in Division Three at the end of the next campaign.

It was not until Nixon moved on that Steve found himself in his favoured right-wing position. His form, particularly at home, was often breathtaking. In December 1974, County crossed the Trent and Steve turned it on in magnificent style. He scored one goal and made another as Forest were defeated 2–0 in what was to be Allan Brown's last game in charge of the 'Reds'. Indirectly 'Flash' had contributed towards Brian Clough becoming the manager at the City Ground!

Strangely though, it would be almost two years before Steve would score another goal for the Magpies, but he was a vital member of the side that enjoyed such a great run in the 1975–76 League Cup competition, playing in the famous wins over Leeds United and Everton.

The decision to put the ever-confident winger on penalty kicks enabled him to kick-start his scoring form again and six of his nine goals in the 1976–77 season came from the spot. Amongst them was the second in County's 2–1 win over Forest, again across the river.

Time finally closed on Steve's Meadow Lane career and after more than 200 first-team appearances he was given a free transfer in August 1978 and allowed to join Derby County, then managed by Tommy Docherty. In and out of the Rams side, he spent three years at the Baseball Ground before being released. Steve's League career ended with a brief spell at AFC Bournemouth.

As so many others have found, consistency is the dividing barrier between the good players and the very best. While it is true that Steve Carter did have some off days, Notts County fans will recall with affection how he twice beat the 'old enemy' and those other magical moments when his mission was simply to entertain.

Gerry Carver

Date of birth: 27 June 1935, Worcester

Notts County record:

Appearances: League 280, FA Cup 12, League Cup 5, Others 0

Goals: League 10, FA Cup 0, League Cup 0, Others 0

Debut: 1 September 1953 v Oldham Athletic (a) won 3–1

Also played for: Boldmere St Michaels, Burton Albion

As the Football League's oldest club, much was made of Notts County's achievement in them becoming the first side to celebrate their centenary. Skipper of the Magpies around that historic period was Gerry Carver, a great club servant who made almost 300 appearances in the Notts midfield.

Gerry's mother and father had moved to Birmingham before World War Two and he began playing his football for an amateur team in Sutton Coldfield called Boldmere St Michaels. Still only 15, he was also invited to train twice a week with Aston Villa. 'Eric Houghton knew me at Villa and when he took over as the Notts manager he pointed out that I'd have a better chance of getting a game there, as there were currently 11 full internationals in the Villa side.'

The youngster saw sense in the offer and moved 'lock, stock and barrel to Nottingham'. 'They put me in digs in Bulwell with Albert Broadbent, who later went on to play for Sheffield Wednesday.' At just 17 years of age he was thrust into the first team and celebrated with a goalscoring debut. 'I know we won 3–1 at Oldham and that Tom Johnston scored the other two goals but I can't remember mine at all – it was a long, long time ago', he remarks.

Like so many other budding footballers, Gerry had to put his career on hold while he completed his national service. 'They put me in the Royal Artillery and sent me to a training camp in Oswestry. There, I served with two other lads who would make their name in the game, Albert Quixall and Ronnie Simpson. I was fortunate that I'd signed for County before my 18th birthday so they were duty bound to keep my contract and pay me a retainer throughout the two years – I think it was £3 a week.'

Returning to the game, Gerry cemented a berth in the County midfield and was a seasoned professional by the time he was made captain by Frank Hill. The 1959–60 season was one of great success, as County clinched promotion by finishing runners-up in the Fourth Division. 'They were great times', says Gerry. 'The fans enjoyed that season and there was always a decent atmosphere at Meadow Lane.'

In 1962 an England XI preparing for the World Cup Finals helped Notts to celebrate their 100th birthday. It was not the best of evenings for Gerry. 'I only lasted a few minutes before going off with a knee ligament injury.'

After more than a decade of service Gerry was eventually released by Notts. 'Brian Clough was manager of Hartlepool at the time and three times he came and tried to persuade me to sign. I'd played at Hartlepool and no way was I going there!' Having rejected Cloughie's advances, there was some irony in the fact that he went on to sign for Burton Albion – managed by Peter Taylor. 'I played at Burton for two years, until Peter went off to join up with Brian.'

With his playing days behind him, Gerry embarked upon a career as a PE teacher in the Prison Service. 'It's funny how they show you respect when they find out you used to be a professional footballer.' After spending 25 years 'behind bars' Gerry and wife Alice, who wed in 1963, settled into retirement in Lowdham, near Nottingham. 'I always look out for County's score and get to see them as often as I can. I'm fortunate that we have plenty of functions for the Ex-Players Association and so I can still keep in touch with many of my old teammates.'

Steve Cherry

Date of birth: 5 August 1960, Nottingham

Notts County record:
Appearances: League 266, FA Cup 14, League Cup 17, Others 31
Debut: 18 February 1989 v Chester City (a) lost 0–1

Also played for: Derby County, Port Vale, Walsall, Plymouth Argyle, Chesterfield, Watford, Rotherham United, Rushden and
                    Diamonds, Mansfield Town, Belper Town, Kidsgrove Athletic

Notts' last line of defence for more than six years was the dependable Steve Cherry. He had already clocked up more than 200 first-team appearances – for Derby County, Walsall and Plymouth Argyle – by the time he signed for a fee of around £70,000.

Whether he imagined that he was joining a progressive club or not, he could not have envisaged that he would be an ever-present as the club rose from the old Division Three to the top flight, and that he would clock up four appearances at Wembley Stadium.

'I played with a lad called Clive Goodyear at Plymouth who left to join Wimbledon and ended up playing in the FA Cup final. I remember wondering if I'd ever get that kind of break.'

The opportunity he had been dreaming of came almost by accident. 'For family reasons I was looking to leave Plymouth and get back nearer to home. Paul Hart was the Chesterfield boss and he gave me the opportunity to go there on loan. I put in a few decent performances but my last game for them was a 3–0 win over Notts County.'

Steve's performance that day impressed Neil Warnock, who stepped in and signed the six-footer – finally completing a deal that almost happened a year earlier. 'John Barnwell had been keen to bring me to Notts but the transfer was shelved after Mick Leonard signed a new contract.'

With Steve on board, Notts were successful in consecutive play-off finals. 'It was great to play at Wembley Stadium at long last and I thought we put in terrific performances both times. I was especially pleased to keep a clean sheet against Tranmere and delighted to get to the end of the Brighton match, as I sustained an ankle injury with 10 minutes to go and had to have my foot strapped up.'

The Warnock era at Meadow Lane is memorable for many reasons but Steve recalls his own particular favourite. 'In the build up to the Manchester City FA Cup match we couldn't train because of the atrocious weather conditions. The manager took us all to Wollaton Park and we spent two or three hours sledging. Cameras were there and I think everyone could see how much fun we were having and how strong our team spirit was.'

Along with the rest of his teammates Steve enjoyed Notts County's European adventure as they twice reached the Anglo-Italian Cup final. 'It was a great experience for us all and it's been interesting to see that some of the clubs we played against have gone on to do well in Serie A over the years. I remember our first trip was actually away at Brescia and we were all looking forward to a bit of sunshine. When we got there they had to clear two feet of snow off the pitch before we could play!'

Steve's love affair with Wembley continued when he featured in an episode of the TV' programme *Record Breakers*. 'We had heats and a final before a couple of England games. Andy Legg won the long-throw competition and I won the furthest throw event, throwing it something like 53 yards. Although Andy's name went into the *Guinness Book of Records*, they didn't include my event in the book. I'll always remember looking up at the Wembley scoreboard though and seeing, "Winner – Steve Cherry".'

After leaving Meadow Lane, Steve's form and fitness ensured he remained very much in demand. A second spell at Plymouth brought him another trip to the Twin Towers for his third play-off final win before he wound down his career in non-League football.

Steve combines work at John Player's in Nottingham with goalkeeper coaching at a number of clubs, including Lincoln City and Hucknall Town.

In the summer of 2005, Steve made a welcome return to the County side, keeping goal in the Sky Sports' 'Masters' tournament.

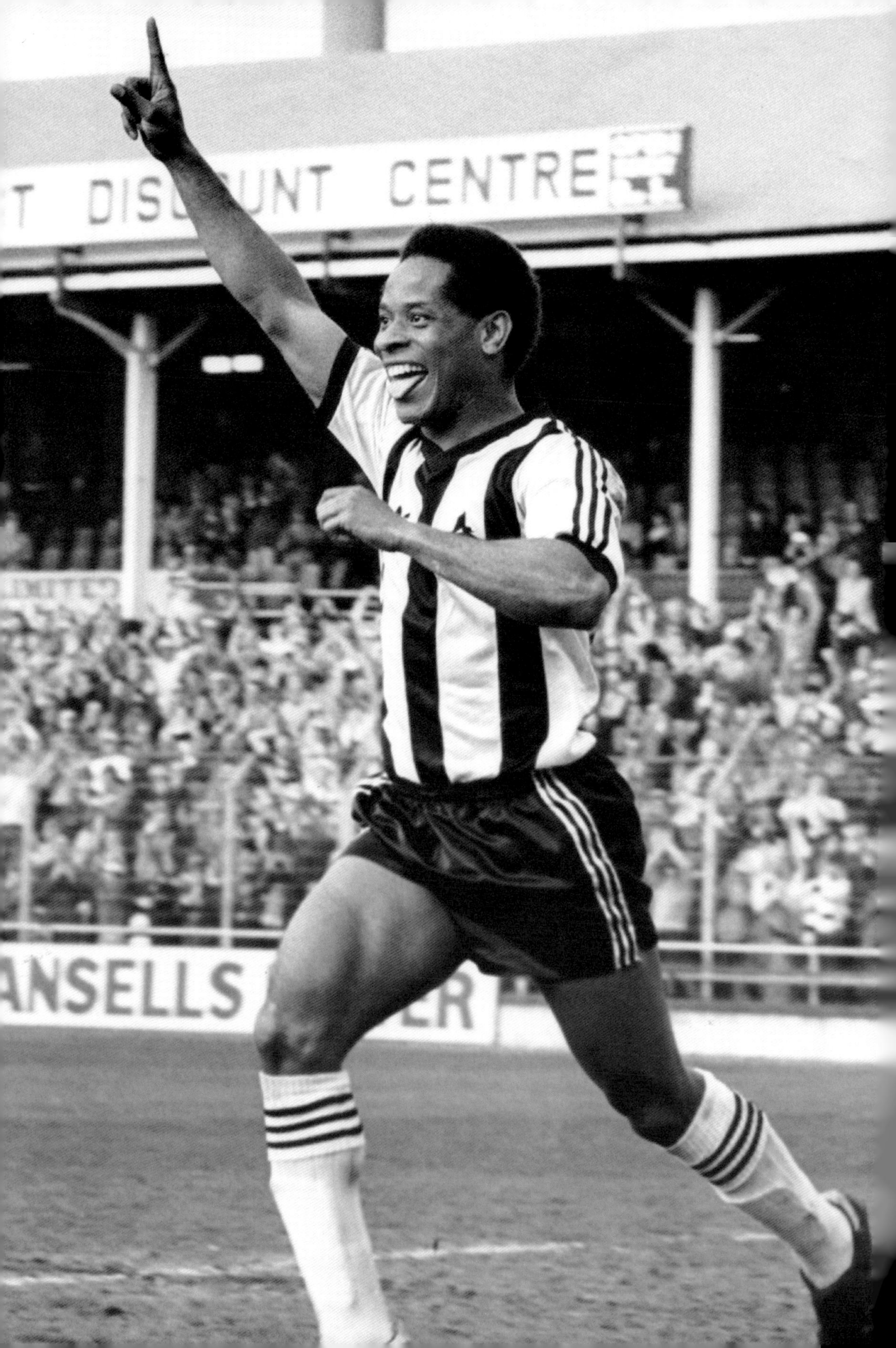

CENTRE
ANSELLS

John Chiedozie

Date of birth: 18 April 1960, Owerri, Nigeria

Notts County record:

Appearances: League 112, FA Cup 8, League Cup 11, Others 0

Goals: League 16, FA Cup 2, League Cup 2, Others 0

Debut: 29 August 1981 v Aston Villa (a) won 1–0

Also played for: Leyton Orient, Tottenham Hotspur, Derby County, Chesterfield, Nigeria (8 caps)

John Chiedozie was an absolute delight to watch – a rascally winger with an eye for goal, a trick or two and decent pace to match. Small in stature but huge of heart, John, at his best, was a match winner.

The Nigerian international moved to Meadow Lane in the summer of 1981, signing for a then-record fee of £600,000 from Leyton Orient. His early years had been difficult, with war in his homeland necessitating that the Chiedozie family had to relocate to England. Life in east London revolved around football for John and he graduated through the O's ranks, turning professional on his 17th birthday.

John's elevation to the first team was spectacular. He had a tough act to follow though, replacing the legendary Laurie Cunningham, who had been the undisputed crowd favourite at Brisbane Road and had departed for West Bromwich Albion.

A series of eye-catching performances and glowing tributes brought John to the attention of the Nigerian coach. Otto Gloria called the young winger into his squad and he made his international debut on 12 July 1980 against Tunisia in a World Cup qualifier. He gained a run in the side, known back then as the 'Green Eagles', and his first international goal came later that year against Tanzania.

John's debut for Notts was the club's first game back in the top flight, the historic 1–0 win at Aston Villa. The new number seven shone that day – and throughout a first season that brought the Magpies a 15th place finish.

Over the next three years, John Chiedozie illuminated Meadow Lane with some dazzling performances, occasionally crowned with some stunning finishes. His final season, the 1983–84 campaign, brought him a best-ever return of 12 League and cup goals. Particularly memorable was a run and finish from the halfway line, which secured a 1–0 win over Middlesbrough in the fifth round of the FA Cup.

That same season he earned a brief recall to his national team, winning an eighth and final cap. John is one of a select band of Notts County players who have appeared in international football.

After three years at Meadow Lane, John moved back to London, joining Spurs. He later returned to the East Midlands, with short stints at both Derby County and Chesterfield. During his stay at Saltergate he did go to Wembley, playing in the side that lost the Division Four play-off final to Cambridge United. Sandwiched between his spells at the two Derbyshire clubs, John briefly returned to Meadow Lane but an injury-hit stay only allowed for one substitute appearance, against Swansea City in March 1990.

After ending his playing days John retired to the New Forest, where he set up his own 'bouncy castle' business.

In 2002, John Chiedozie was deservedly honoured by the Nigerian President, Olusegan Obesanjo, who presented him with the Officer of the Order of Niger for services to Nigerian football.

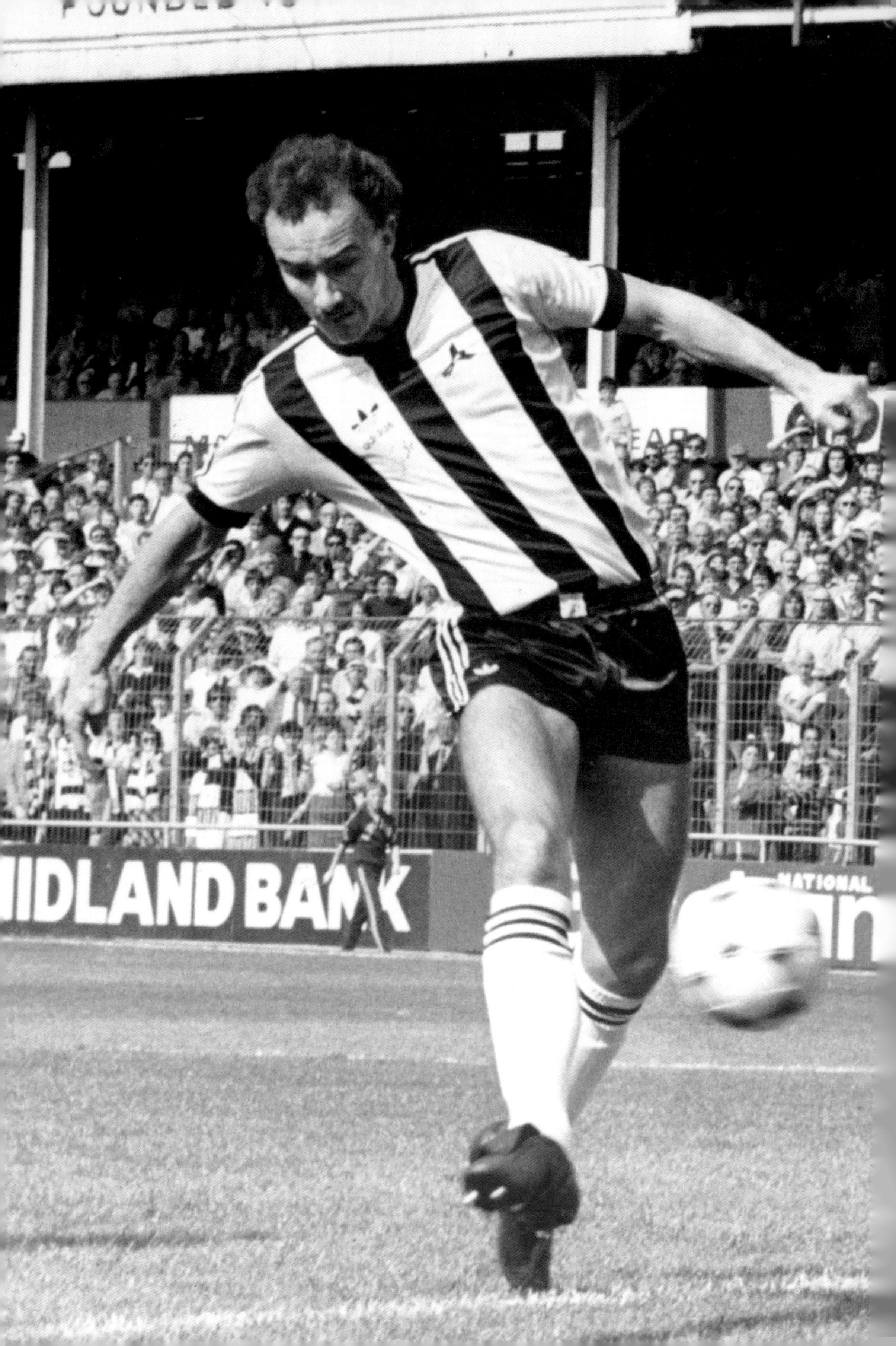
IDLAND BA
NATIONAL

Trevor Christie

Date of birth: 28 February 1959, Cresswell, Northumberland

Notts County record:

Appearances: League 186, FA Cup 10, League Cup 20, Others 10

Goals: League 63, FA Cup 3, League Cup 10, Others 3

Debut: 4 August 1979 v Mansfield Town (a) won 1–0 (Anglo-Scottish Cup)

Also played for: Leicester City, Nottingham Forest, Derby County, Manchester City, Walsall, Mansfield Town, Kettering Town, VS Rugby, Hucknall Town, Arnold Town, Wollaton

Goals win matches – and ultimately titles. Although no one will dispute that County's promotion season of 1980–81 was a real team effort, the honour of being top goalscorer went to Trevor Christie.

Although his total of 21 goals included seven in the cup, Trevor knew just when to put on a show. He scored the first at Stamford Bridge on the day that top-flight football was secured and he claimed another, three days later, as County ended the season in celebratory style at home to Cambridge United.

He had joined Notts in 1979 after completing a £60,000 move from Leicester City. Like all good strikers, he was keen to get off the mark and he did so on his debut. The Anglo-Scottish Cup competition began during pre-season and County's opening fixture in this prestigious affair saw them travel to Field Mill to face Mansfield Town. Trevor's goal gave the Magpies a 1–0 win.

Once the League season commenced Trevor broke his duck in the second match, away at Shrewsbury, and went on to score a total of 10 for the season.

Big and strong, Trevor certainly gave the Notts attack a physical edge. Brave in the challenge and lethal in the air, his signing already looked to be a decent bit of business. His form remained consistent throughout the promotion season and there was no doubt he would acquit himself well at the higher level.

Trevor scored a dozen goals as Notts accustomed themselves to life in the old First Division. Amongst his haul was a hat-trick against Brighton and goals in both League matches against Nottingham Forest. If Brian Clough's side had not already seen enough of Trevor, they were made to suffer at his hands again when the sides met in a thriller at Meadow Lane in December 1982. Two goals each at the interval, Trevor's winner ensured the town was painted black and white that night. In three consecutive local derbies County's centre-forward had delivered against their fiercest rivals.

The 1983–84 season was Trevor's last with the Magpies but he started and ended it in style. On the opening day of the campaign he had the satisfaction of scoring another hat-trick, at Filbert Street, against his former side Leicester City.

By the spring, County were on their way out of the top flight and, despite a 3–1 defeat against Southampton on the final afternoon, it was Trevor who got the Notts goal. Not only was it the club's last score in Division One for a few years, it also marked his final appearance. Fittingly, the supporters acknowledged Trevor's performance, making him joint Player of the Year, alongside John Chiedozie.

After his earlier feats against them it was perhaps no surprise when Forest stepped in to snap up the striker and keep him in Division One. Later he joined Mansfield Town, completing the set of playing for all three of Nottinghamshire's League clubs. There is no doubt his best years were spent with the Magpies and whether he was barging past a struggling defender or coolly slotting home a penalty kick, his ability to produce when it mattered most will ensure he always remains a terrace hero.

Arthur Clamp

Date of birth: 1 May 1884, Sneinton, Notts

Died: 19 September 1918

Notts County record:

Appearances: League 275, FA Cup 14

Goals: League 3, FA Cup 0

Debut: 29 December 1906 v Bolton Wanderers (a) drew 0–0

Also played for: Sneinton

The esteem in which Arthur Clamp was held was never better illustrated than on the day of his funeral. Killed tragically early, from wounds received during World War One, Arthur's final journey through the streets of Nottingham was witnessed by thousands of tearful supporters.

Arthur had joined Notts in the 1906–07 season from his local club, Sneinton. The blonde-haired youngster cut quite a dashing figure and was hugely popular with teammates and supporters alike. Although not a towering six-footer, Arthur had good attributes for a centre-half. He was dependable in the air, determined in the tackle and a fine distributor of the ball. He rarely ventured upfield, as is evident by his meagre goal return. The first of just three career strikes came shortly after he joined the club, at home to Woolwich Arsenal.

The Magpies had gained promotion to the top flight of the Football League at the end of the 1896–97 season, so by the time of Arthur's arrival at the club, they were a consolidated middle-of-the-table team.

Team selection was rarely an issue as the Notts back line virtually picked itself during this period of the club's history – Albert Iremonger was an automatic choice in goal, Herbert Morley and John Montgomery the full-backs and Teddy Emberton and Reuben Craythorne the wing-halves. All played over 250 times for the club in a defensive unit completed by the talented Clamp, who went on to make 275 League appearances for the club. Form and fitness were taken for granted as Arthur featured in every League game from 19 October 1907 until 28 January 1911, a sequence of 128 matches.

The summer of 1910 saw Notts move across the river from their old headquarters at the Trent Bridge Cricket Ground to their present site on Meadow Lane. Arthur featured in both the last game at the old site and the first at the new venue, a 1–1 draw against Nottingham Forest. Also the same year, the club undertook their first tour abroad, a three-match trip to Denmark. Two games were won, with the other being drawn.

Notts' tenure in the First Division was broken by relegation at the end of the 1912–13 term, but immediately restored with promotion as champions the following season.

The outbreak of World War One meant a cessation of the Football League, with Arthur playing in Notts' final game, a 2–0 home victory over Chelsea on 28 April 1915. He played several times for the club's Midland League side the following year, before going away to fight for his country.

World War One claimed the lives of so many young men, among them one of County's greatest-ever servants. After sustaining injuries on the Western Front, Arthur Clamp was brought home to a military hospital in Newcastle-under-Lyme, where he died on 19 September 1918, aged just 34.

After his funeral cortège passed through the streets of the city, Arthur was buried at Sneinton Parish Church.

Bill Corkhill

Date of birth: 23 April 1910, Belfast
Died: 9 August 1978

Notts County record:
Appearances: League 284, FA Cup 20, Others 4
Goals: League 9, FA Cup 2, Others 0
Debut: 6 February 1932 v Barnsley (a) drew 1–1

Also played for: Northern Nomads, Marine, Cardiff City
Managed: Scunthorpe United, Bradford Park Avenue, Hastings United

In terms of longevity, Bill Corkhill's connection with Notts spanned almost 20 years. When he played his final game for the club, a 2–1 defeat away at Barnsley on 12 September 1951, he was 41 years 142 days old, the most senior outfield player ever to represent the club. Another interesting statistic is that Bill scored two goals in the FA Cup competition for Notts but they were in January 1933 and January 1948 – 15 years apart!

Bill's best years as a footballer, like so many of his generation, were interrupted by World War Two. Although he had joined Cardiff City before the conflict began, he returned to Meadow Lane afterwards and, along with Bill Fallon, is one of only two players to play either side of the hostilities.

The young Irishman joined Notts from Marine, a non-League club on Merseyside. Playing mainly at right-half he flitted in and out of the side over his first couple of seasons. A first goal for the club came in the FA Cup competition, fittingly back on Merseyside against Tranmere Rovers.

He really began to establish himself as a regular during the 1934–35 season. Although the campaign ended in the disappointment of relegation from the old Second Division, the development of Bill was viewed as a major bonus. Over the course of the next three seasons he rarely missed a game as Notts chased promotion. Second in 1936–37 was as near as they came. During the summer of 1938, Bill bade farewell to his life and friends in Nottingham and signed for Cardiff City for what turned out to be just one season.

During the war Bill frequently 'guested' for Notts, so it was no real surprise when he rejoined them in time for the peacetime resurrection of the Football League. Bill's last League appearance at Meadow Lane, in 1938, had attracted just 2,828 fans. The first game after the war was attended by a crowd of 28,779 as the Nottingham public came out in force to welcome their heroes.

Switching between the half-back and full-back positions, Bill's versatility came in useful, never more so than on 21 December 1946. The particularly bad winter was playing havoc with the trains and goalkeeper Harry Brown, who lived in London, was unable to arrive for a match at Walsall. Bill went in goal, but there was to be no happy ending as County succumbed 2–0.

Understandably Bill's appearances in the side lessened as he reached his late thirties but he was still able to make a valuable contribution to the side when he spent a brief spell as the club's trainer. During the promotion-winning campaign of 1949–50 he played just once but further appearances over the next couple of seasons took him into the record books, second only to 'keeper Albert Iremonger in terms of age.

Bill joined Scunthorpe United as their manager in 1952 and assembled a side that twice narrowly missed out on promotion, as well as embarking on a couple of headline-grabbing FA Cup runs. Feeling he had taken the club as far as he could, he resigned in May 1956 and took up a similar position with Bradford Park Avenue. Unable to command the same level of fulfilment at Bradford, he left after only 18 months. After spending a brief period at Hastings United he became senior coach to the Notts FA.

In later life Bill Corkhill became a licensee in Nottingham before sadly passing away in 1978.

Reuben Craythorne

Date of birth: 21 January 1882, Small Heath, Birmingham
Died: 21 October 1953

Notts County record:
Appearances: League 282, FA Cup 14
Goals: League 12, FA Cup 0
Debut: 10 September 1904 v Small Heath (a) won 2–1

Also played for: Coventry City, Darlington

After enjoying a couple of FA Cup final appearances and a promotion to the top flight, Notts County ended the 19th century confident of more success. All seemed well when they finished third in the 1900–01 season, thereby matching their highest ever League placing. Sadly, such heights were not reached again as the club began a steady fall from grace. It would be nine long years before County finished inside the top 10. Nevertheless, several decent players represented the club during this period – amongst them, Reuben Craythorne.

'Ben' was signed from Coventry City, where he had played as an inside-forward. He made his debut in September 1904 and scored the winning goal in a 2–1 victory over Small Heath. He added a further three goals that season but, overall, it was a disastrous campaign in terms of results. Just five wins, with only one at home, ensured that the club would finish bottom of the 18 First Division clubs. Fearing relegation, Notts were reprieved when the League announced that it was to increase the size of the top flight by two extra clubs and thereby extend their occupation of Division One.

Collectively, Notts fared little better the next season. Knocked out of the cup in the first round and 16th in the League, it was a bleak period for the fans, although home attendances at the Trent Bridge Cricket Ground were regularly over the 10,000 mark. By this stage of his career Ben had been converted to left-half and he was an ever-present in the number six jersey during the 1905–06 season. This had become his favoured position, although he volunteered for a new role on Boxing Day 1906.

Regular goalkeeper Albert Iremonger was unavailable. His deputy, Bob Suter, was delayed by rail travel so Ben went in goal for an away match at Sheffield United. Although he acquitted himself well, there was to be no fairytale ending, as the Blades ran out 2–1 winners.

Over the course of the next four years Craythorne's consistency was instrumental in Notts remaining in the top flight. Although international recognition did not fall his way, he was selected to represent the Football League against the Irish League in the 1906–07 season.

The summer of 1910 was a transitional one for Notts. They went on their first overseas tour – a three-match trip to Denmark. Their return coincided with a move across the river, to their new home. Having participated in the club's last League fixture at Trent Bridge, Ben was also a member of the side that played against Nottingham Forest in the first ever match at Meadow Lane. On 3 September 1910 an estimated attendance of 28,000 packed into the new 'County Ground', as it was called, to see the local rivals fiercely contest a 1–1 draw.

The stocky left-footer took his appearance tally for Notts towards the 300 game mark before he left to join Darlington during the 1912–13 season.

Although his time at Notts was not complemented by a huge haul of medals, Reuben Craythorne was a loyal servant to the club and widely regarded as one of the finest half-backs of his generation.

Harry Cursham

Date of birth: 27 November 1859, Wilford

Died: 6 August 1941

Notts County record:

Appearances: League 9, FA Cup 36, Others 177

Goals: League 2, FA Cup 49, Others 158

Debut: 13 October 1877 v Stoke (h) won 4–1

Also played for: Corinthians, Thursday Wanderers (Sheffield), Grantham, England (8 caps), Nottinghamshire County Cricket Club

It is a fairly safe bet that only the keenest of football statisticians would know who has scored the most goals in the history of the FA Cup competition.

Between 1877 and 1889 Harry Cursham netted 49 cup goals, all of them for Notts County. He actually netted another couple in a match that was declared void after a protest and later ordered to be replayed.

His brothers Arthur and Charles also played for Notts – indeed the former was regarded as one of the most talented players of his generation, captaining club and country before retiring to Florida in 1884 and meeting an untimely death, at the age of 31, after contracting malaria.

Harry Cursham was one of the earliest true 'stars' of Notts County. Towards the end of his career he switched to defence but for the most part he played either as the centre-forward or out on the flank where, fleet of foot, he possessed a keen eye for goal and a penchant for shooting at every opportunity.

He succeeded his siblings into the County line-up at the start of the 1877–78 season and gave an indication of what was to come by firing a hat-trick, at home to Stoke, on his debut. In an era where high scores were not uncommon, Harry delighted in scoring his goals in multiples. He claimed a five and a four in his first season, as well as recording his maiden goal in the FA Cup, a competition he was to revel in over the next dozen seasons.

Amongst his goal-scoring exploits for Notts, Harry hit six in an 11–1 'stroll' against Wednesbury Strollers in 1881 and four in the 15–0 massacre over Rotherham Town four years later, a result which remains the club's record margin of victory.

Harry won the first of eight international caps in 1880, when he was picked to play for England against Wales. In the history of the game no other Notts County player has played as many times for England as Harry did. Typically, the striker carried his club form into the international arena. His five goals included a hat-trick in an 8–1 victory over Ireland in Belfast in February 1884.

Harry simply loved scoring hat-tricks, a prestigious feat in those days. He scored over 20 of them for Notts County but was unable to record one in the Football League.

As it began its inaugural season in 1888/89, Harry was nearing the end of his career. He played in just eight matches that year and then reappeared for the final time, playing at right-back, two years later.

Also a keen cricketer, Harry was good enough to play a couple of first-class games for Notts – but they were spread over a period of 24 years. The first was in 1880 and the second in 1904 when he was invited to skipper the side against the South African touring side.

Tommy Deans

Date of birth: 7 January 1922, Shieldhill, Lanarkshire

Died: 30 October 2000

Notts County record:

Appearances: League 239, FA Cup 13

Goals: League 0, FA Cup 0

Debut: 8 October 1949 v Newport County (a) drew 1–1

Also played for: Clyde, Boston United, Wisbech Town, Grantham Town

What a great full-back Tommy Deans was. Equally capable on either side of the defence, he was a no-nonsense tackler and inspirational leader.

Thomas Sneddon Deans joined Notts in October 1949, signing for £7,500 from Scottish side Clyde, where he had made 45 League appearances. He went straight into a Notts side bubbling with confidence and riding high at the top of the Division Three South table. Meadow Lane was packed for every home game as Lawton, Sewell and co. swept all before them. During a memorable season for everyone connected with the club, neighbours Nottingham Forest were defeated both home and away. Apart from in three matches, where he played at left-back, Tommy wore the number two jersey and clocked up 29 appearances to justify his transfer fee and qualify for a championship medal.

Tommy was no more than average height but he was a fiercely competitive opponent. Stocky in build, he had a good turn of pace and was more than a match for any winger of the day. During a six-year stretch, he missed only the occasional game through injury and twice completed a season as an ever-present member of the side.

Sadly for Tommy, he did not manage to register a single goal during his professional career, either side of the border. He maintained a philosophy of being a defender first and rarely ventured forward, even for set-pieces.

Tommy's popularity in the dressing room saw him promoted to club skipper in time for County's momentous FA Cup run during the 1954–55 season. After wins over Middlesbrough and Sheffield Wednesday, Notts were handed a plum fifth-round tie at home to Chelsea. A single goal by Albert Broadbent was enough for victory over a side who were en route to the First Division title.

Tommy's Magpies were in the sixth round for the first time since 1922. A ground record crowd of 47,310 squeezed into Meadow Lane but, ultimately, went home disappointed as York City defied their Third Division status to win the match 1–0. Reaching the semi-finals or better would have been a marvellous way for Tommy to bring down the curtain on a fabulous spell with Notts. As it was he remained at the club for a further year, compiling just 21 appearances during the season. His final match was a home defeat against Hull City in March 1956.

After leaving County, Tom joined the non-League scene, spending a season with Boston United. He played in 45 League matches, plus another couple of FA Cup-ties, but a first senior goal still eluded him.

Paul Devlin

Date of birth: 14 April 1972, Birmingham

Notts County record:
Appearances: League 146, FA Cup 8, League Cup 12, Others 19
Goals: League 25, FA Cup 1, League Cup 1, Others 4
Debut: 11 April 1992 v Coventry City (h) won 1–0

Also played for: Stafford Rangers, Birmingham City, Sheffield United, Watford, Scotland (10 caps)

It is always a delight to watch a tricky wingman in full flight and on his day Paul Devlin was up amongst the best.

Paul was brought to Meadow Lane by Neil Warnock but it was another manager with Notts connections who nearly nipped in to sign him. 'I'd been doing well for Stafford and I remember taking a day off work. The phone went and it was Howard Wilkinson inviting me to go to Leeds for a trial. Naturally I was fairly excited but then I got another call, with the caller claiming to be Neil Warnock. I suddenly twigged that it might be my mates trying to wind me up.'

Both calls turned out to be genuine and Paul did speak to Leeds but he was more impressed with what he saw and heard at County and he was happy to sign. 'Notts were still in the old First Division at the time and I felt at home straight away. Training and the reserve games went well and then I was given my debut against Coventry City. In five or six weeks I'd gone from working on a building site to playing in the top flight. I was up against Kenny Sansom, one of England's most successful full-backs. It was a red hot day but we won and I felt I did alright.'

'Dev' settled into life as a full-time professional and staked a permanent place in the side. His first goal came away against Grimsby. 'It was a significant moment to get my first goal but it was a strange day weather-wise. They showed the pictures on *Central News* – we were playing on a green pitch in bright sunshine then later we were playing on a white surface in a snow blizzard.' The match ended 3–3 and Paul still remembers his goal. 'The ball came out of the box to me. I feinted to shoot, cut inside and fired it low across the 'keeper.'

With Notts now in the second tier of the English game, they were able to experience some European football. 'The Anglo-Italian Cup was a much-maligned tournament but we thoroughly enjoyed it. It was a welcome break from the League and the matches in Italy were certainly a novelty for some of us younger players.' Successive finals meant two big days out at Wembley. 'It was fantastic to play there, although we were bitterly disappointed to lose against Brescia. To go back the year after and win made it even sweeter.'

Paul has lots of happy memories from his time with Notts, particularly the famous 2–1 win over Forest. 'That was such a big match for us. We knew the fans were desperate for us to do well and when Charlie Palmer scored, the place went wild.' The photos of Palmer celebrating, immediately after his goal, show 'Dev' in hot pursuit. 'I've never seen Charlie run so fast – he was brilliant to me when I went to the club, a great help, and I was so pleased for him then.'

Paul actually top scored for Notts in the 1994–95 season with 12 – 'Mick Walker and Russell Slade were always encouraging me to shoot more' – and inevitably clubs began to take notice. In February 1996 he signed for the first of two spells with Birmingham City for £250,000. He later rejoined Neil Warnock at Sheffield United and even spent a five-match loan spell back with Notts in 1998.

His second period at St Andrews brought some belated international recognition. 'I have to admit I thought the opportunity had passed me by. I'd turned 30 when Berti Vogts called and selected me to play for Scotland. My dad is from Coatbridge and all the family are Celtic fans, so you can imagine my delight. I don't think I was playing any better then than at any other time in my career but I was getting noticed because I was playing in the Premier League.'

Paul's debut in the blue of Scotland came at Easter Road against Canada in October 2002. Nine other caps soon followed to delight the jinking winger. 'It was great to win 10 caps for my country but I wished it had happened five years earlier.'

The 2004–05 season was particularly memorable for Paul for all the wrong reasons. On the books of Watford, his season finished early with a toe injury. 'After 13 years in the game I had to undergo my first operation – something of a record for a footballer.'

Mark Draper

Date of birth: 11 November 1970, Long Eaton

Notts County record:

Appearances: League 222, FA Cup 10, League Cup 15, Others 23
Goals: League 40, FA Cup 2, League Cup 2, Others 5
Debut: 6 September 1988 v Mansfield Town (a) lost 0–1 (League Cup)

Also played for: Leicester City, Aston Villa, Rayo Vallecano (Spain), Southampton

Mark Draper was one of the most stylish midfielders ever to wear Notts County's famous stripes. Between 1988 and 1994 he clocked up 270 first-team appearances and twice played at Wembley for the club.

His association with the Magpies began at an early age, as he confesses. 'I was involved with them, really, from about the age of 10 or 11. I've got to admit to a slight leaning toward the other team in the city in those days – but that soon changed!'

Graduating through the youth team ranks, Mark's potential ensured that his dreams of becoming a professional footballer would become a reality. 'I actually did my first full pre-season, while I was still at school.' His debut was relatively low key. Leading 5–0 from the home match, he was introduced into the side for a second leg League Cup-tie away at Mansfield Town.

'Drapes' made 20 League appearances in his first season and became more established the second year. The signing of Dean Thomas meant that he often missed out towards the end of the 1989–90 campaign, including a place in the play-off final. 'I can honestly say that I wasn't too upset. I was on the bench and didn't get on but we knew we were all in it together. The manager had built up such a great team spirit – and at just 19 I thought I had time on my side.'

This was a prophetic judgement because just 12 months later Mark was given his Wembley debut in the play-off final against Brighton. 'It just flew by and I can't recall too much about the match. I know the experience of the previous year helped enormously because I knew what to expect. We were so confident – there was never any thought of us losing.'

The fixture list was not too kind to Notts but at least Mark will always remember his first match in the top flight. 'On the opening day we played Manchester United at Old Trafford. Although we lost 2–0 I thought we did alright. The manager had made the decision to stick with the players who'd got us up – that was fair enough. Really, though, we didn't sign enough quality to keep us in the division and it was always going to be a struggle.'

Mark had enjoyed pitting his skills against the best in the land and eventually moved on to play in the Premiership. Before then, he was able to sample 'European football' in a Notts shirt and score a goal he still gets asked about. 'The Anglo-Italian Cup competition was something of a novelty for us. Trips abroad were great for morale and it was pleasing to have a little bit of success.'

Although Notts lost the 1994 final to Brescia, it did give Mark another opportunity to appear at 'the venue of legends'. Like most of his teammates, there was one abiding memory of that trip to Wembley. 'I'll never understand what Gheorghe Hagi was doing playing for them. He was absolutely brilliant.'

As a provider, Mark will be remembered for the free-kick which enabled Charlie Palmer to score his famous winner against Forest. As a scorer, though, one County goal stands out above all others. 'Last day of the season – against Sunderland at home. It was a sunny day and a full house are there because we have to win to stay up. Dean Thomas crossed it and I hit a volley from the edge of the box which flew into the top corner.'

In the summer of 1994, Mark signed for Leicester City and had further spells at Villa and Southampton, as well as a short loan spell in Spain with Rayo Vallecano. Injury curtailed his career but meant that he was able to concentrate on another couple of projects. 'I'm working on my golf and want to get my handicap right down, and I've gone into business with Dean Richards, a former clubmate at Southampton, and we're involved in overseas property development.'

Still living locally, Mark keeps a close eye on the fortunes of his former club. 'I had a terrific six or seven years on the staff at Notts and I'd love to see them doing well again.'

Jack Dunnett

Date of birth: 24 June 1922, Glasgow

Notts County record:
Chairman: 1969–1988

Throughout Notts County's rise from the depths of the Fourth Division to the promised land of Division One, the man at the helm was chairman Jack Dunnett. As the expectations of the supporters intensified, Jack would often issue a rallying cry, urging the fans to keep on turning up to Meadow Lane.

'A football club has to have a good fan base', says Jack. 'Really there's no point to it if you don't have supporters wishing you on. I was always happy to put some money into the club to assist with purchasing players but it only goes so far before it needs renewing, so you've got more money to buy more players.'

Jack knew his limitations. 'I did my sums. At the time we had a potential catchment area of 270,000 people, perhaps stretching it to 350,000 when you went into outlying districts. There is no other city in Britain with just that many potential supporters who run two football teams. Nottingham is totally unique in that respect. Look at cities like Sunderland and Newcastle, who have over a million people each but just one football club.'

A qualified solicitor, Jack loved his football and was living in London when he decided to become involved with a club. 'I didn't really want to follow one of the "fashionable" teams, like Spurs or Arsenal, and thought Brentford was ideal. I talked to the directors and they invited me on to the board. I was about 39 or 40 years old at the time but the rest of the directors were in their seventies. After just a short time on the board the chairman addressed a meeting and said, "I've been looking for somebody younger to take over and I feel we've got someone now who can take over." Naturally I was very flattered.'

Jack became the Labour MP for Nottingham Central (after demarcation the ward was later known as Nottingham East) and understandably was spending more and more of his time in the city.

'The Notts County board knew of my involvement with Brentford but they gave me a season ticket for the directors' box and made it clear I would be very welcome should I wish to join the board at Meadow Lane. I felt that Brentford weren't really going anywhere as there was a definite lack of enthusiasm from the other board members, so when I received an offer for my shares I decided to leave and accept the invitation to join the set-up at Notts.'

On 13 March 1967, Jack Dunnett became a director and very soon found himself in the chair. 'Bill Hopcroft was the chairman but when he had a stroke I was asked to take over in his absence. After his convalescence he felt I'd done a good job and asked me to take over permanently.'

It is fair to say that there was plenty of work to be done. 'The main task was to reorganise the finances. Believe it or not, the club had gone through so many managers in such a short time that they were still paying four of them off!'

Acquiring the next manager also fell into Jack's priority list. 'During my time at Brentford I'd been terribly impressed by Jimmy Sirrel. He'd been the trainer then but took over as manager after I'd left. He was a hard worker and hadn't got a contract. I spoke to Jimmy and knew he could do a great job with very little money to spend. I remember the *Evening Post* headline, "Jimmy Who?" '

The rapport between the two Scotsmen was an integral part of Notts County's success, culminating in promotion to the top flight. 'The day we won at Chelsea must rank as the most memorable but it was a great achievement to not only go up, but to stay there for three years as well.'

During the mid-1970s Stuart Burgan became County's Commercial Manager and he recalls his old boss with affection. 'Jack was always busy and very hard working. He would usually just come to the club on Fridays but he was totally dedicated and a man you just had to respect. His board meetings became legendary.'

Jack explains about the system he employed. 'Most football clubs have a board meeting just about every other week. We would talk often and see each other at games and any issues were resolved there and then. Our annual board meeting was therefore a formality and one was famously timed at being just four and a half minutes long.'

Jack's standing continued to rise within the game. In 1977, at the age of 55, he was elected on to the management committee of the Football League. Four years later he received the ultimate accolade when he became President.

Over a 19-year period Jack Dunnett served Notts County with honest endeavour and total commitment – and for that the fans will always be grateful.

Dick Edwards

Date of birth: 20 November 1942, Kirkby-in-Ashfield, Notts

Notts County record:

Appearances: League 221, FA Cup 10, League Cup 14

Goals: League 20, FA Cup 0, League Cup 1

Debut: 26 December 1959 v Rochdale (h) won 2–1

Also played for: East Kirkby Welfare Juniors, Mansfield Town, Torquay United, Aston Villa, Bath City, Brixham

For the modern day footballer the close-season break is viewed as a time to cruise around the Mediterranean or soak up the sun in the Caribbean. Players of a different era had to find work to supplement their income but that certainly did not worry Dick Edwards. 'I left school at 15 and went to work down the pit at Newstead Colliery. So when I got a chance to play football I was so grateful and so determined to make the most of it. Other apprentices moaned about having to clean the boots of the first-teamers but I loved it!'

Dick had played his junior football for his local side, East Kirkby Miners Welfare but was also good enough to be on Nottingham Forest's books. 'I was determined not to work down the pit for long so I went to see Billy Walker, the Forest manager, with my father. He said that he still wasn't sure about me. Notts County heard and they said they'd take me on. I was even more pleased about this because they were the team I supported.'

The year 1959 really was one to remember for Dick, as he recalls. 'In the space of 10 months I went from a job at the colliery into professional football, earned a call-up to the England Under-18 side and made my first-team debut!'

Dick was still only 17 when he broke into the Notts team for the first time and his footballing future looked assured. He needed to find work during the summer though. 'We had three months off and I landed a job as a Butlin's "Red Coat". I would either go to Skegness or Ayr in Scotland. I'd started playing the guitar and would take it to Meadow Lane and after training would accompany Jack Wheeler on his banjo. At Butlin's I got used to going on the stage and entertaining properly.'

During one summer break Dick met a celebrated guest. 'One year at Ayr, the great Bill Shankly came and stayed. When we played football I made sure he was on my side!'

Predominantly a right-back, Dick played in virtually every position during his career, even going in goal during a later spell with Mansfield. It was in the number two jersey that he settled into the Magpies side and began to attract attention. In the centenary season of 1962, Notts played host to an England XI and Dick was entrusted with marking Peter Thompson, the Preston left-winger who later starred for Liverpool. 'We lost 3–1 but I did OK – after the match they gave us a special commemorative medal which turned out to be the only thing I won in 18 years in the game!'

Occasionally Dick would be given the chance to stretch his legs, playing up front. One afternoon at Brighton he scored twice in the first half and felt an outstanding ambition was within reach. 'I'd always fancied scoring a hat-trick and things were going well, then at half-time they told me that Tony Bircumshaw was injured so I was being moved to left-back!'

Jeff Astle was a Notts teammate at the time and the pair became firm buddies. 'I was best man at Jeff's wedding. He was a good friend and a smashing bloke.'

After eight years at Meadow Lane, Dick moved on and served Mansfield Town, Aston Villa and Torquay United with many years of sterling service. His days in the holiday camps had stood him in good stead though as he built up a career for himself as a country music singer and all-round entertainer. 'Sometimes we go out as a duo, sometimes there are three of us, but we're called The Dick Edwards Trio and I get to sing and tell a few jokes. Over the years we've done a CD or two and my love of Notts County usually gets a mention somewhere on the album!'

Based back in his home town of Kirkby-in-Ashfield, Dick still performs several times a week but continues to follow the fortunes of the Magpies. 'As far as I'm concerned, they'll always be my club and I'm delighted that they've really looked after me whenever I've gone back.'

Teddy Emberton

Date of birth: 23 June 1884, Titchmarch, Northants

Died: 21 December 1957

Notts County record:

Appearances: League 365, FA Cup 17

Goals: League 2, FA Cup 1

Debut: 15 October 1904 v Preston North End (a) lost 1–3

Also played for: Stafford Rangers

It is rare in the modern game for a footballer to remain at the same club for a decade or more. A century ago it was more common, although players still had to merit their place on the field.

When Notts brought a young right-half into their ranks in the autumn of 1904, they could not have envisaged the sterling service that he would give them. Fred 'Teddy' Emberton features high among the top 10 of Notts County's all-time appearance-makers – and deservedly so.

As a young schoolboy Teddy had developed a love of football that earned him a chance with Stafford Rangers. His potential was evident and he accepted an opportunity to move to Nottingham to join Notts. His debut season coincided with the club finishing at the bottom of the table but they earned a reprieve from relegation by the Football League. Instead, two more sides were added to Division One and the threat of relegation was removed for one season.

Apart from his playing ability Teddy was a likeable young man and immensely popular with his teammates and the supporters. The Notts half-back unit at the time comprised of Teddy, Arthur Clamp and Reuben Craythorne – three solid, dependable performers who each made in excess of 280 appearances for the club.

At the conclusion of the 1909–10 season Teddy played in Notts County's final home match at Trent Bridge, against champions Aston Villa, and then went to Denmark on the first overseas tour undertaken by the club.

During the close season there was a switch of premises as Notts moved from Trent Bridge to their new headquarters on Meadow Lane. The new venue was initially called 'The County Ground' and its debut match, on 3 September 1910, was scripted to perfection - a Division One local derby against Nottingham Forest. Honours were even as the game finished 1–1 and for a while Teddy was credited with the Notts goal. A shot from Bill Matthews appeared to deflect in off the half-back but afterwards Emberton admitted the ball had not touched him, so he was denied a place in the record books as the scorer of Notts first goal at their new home.

Considering Teddy's scoring record, it is perhaps testimony to the man that he did not try and claim the goal. In 382 first-team matches for Notts, he only found the net on three occasions. His first goal for the club came in the second round of the FA Cup in 1906, against Burslem Port Vale. His only two League goals came seven years apart – against Bury in October 1907 and then at Chelsea in November 1914.

After 16 years of top-flight football, Notts had suffered relegation at the end of the 1912–13 season but bounced back at the first time of asking, winning Division Two by four clear points. Teddy had been an ever-present throughout the promotion campaign but global events were soon to overtake sporting interests. With the world at war, League football was put on hold at the end of the 1914–15 season.

Fred Emberton played his 365th and final League match for Notts on 3 April 1915 – bowing out on a losing note, with a 1–3 defeat at Bradford City.

Steve Finnan

Date of birth: 20 April 1976, Limerick

Notts County record:

Appearances: League 97, FA Cup 6, League Cup 4, Others 3
Goals: League 7, FA Cup 1, League Cup 0, Others 1
Debut: 6 March 1996 v Walsall (h) won 2-1

Also played for: Welling United, Birmingham City, Fulham, Liverpool, Republic of Ireland (35 caps – to end of 2004–05 season)

In every sense, it is a fair distance from Meadow Lane to a Champions League final in Istanbul but that is the journey undertaken by Steve Finnan.

It is probably fair to admit that Notts County was just a stepping-stone for Steve on his way to bigger and better things but, despite that observation, he was an outstanding success during his time with the club.

He first donned the black and white stripes towards the end of the 1995–96 season, when Birmingham City let him out on loan. Playing as a right-sided midfielder, his impact was impressive. A couple of early goals for his new club helped County into the end-of-season Division Two play-offs and then another against Crewe Alexandra in the semi-final contributed towards the Magpies heading off for another big day out at Wembley.

It certainly was not third time lucky for Notts though – having won twice before at the old stadium under Neil Warnock, they lost a play-off final for the first time with Colin Murphy's side going down to Bradford City. 'Even playing at Wembley wasn't any consolation', said Steve afterwards. 'We were all bitterly disappointed by our performance on the day.'

Despite the loss it was clear that the two-month experience had been of benefit to both parties and Notts and the player were keen to make the move permanent. A deal of £300,000 was agreed and Steve became a Magpie early the following season. For most of the next two years he was a virtual ever-present and under Sam Allardyce he blossomed into a very accomplished player.

The hurt of the play-off final was partially overcome when Notts romped to the Division Three championship in 1997–98. Having dropped to the bottom division, the Magpies stormed to success with 'Finns' playing in all but two of the matches and contributing five important goals.

His performances were understandably beginning to attract headlines and draw admirers. It was not a surprise when an offer was made that was just too good to refuse. Fulham manager Kevin Keegan, backed by Mohammed Al-Fayed's cheque book, signed him for £600,000 in November 1998.

Steve had been converted to full-back by now and he proved to be an astute signing as he helped Fulham to successive promotions and a place in the big time. Others were watching his advancement and a full call-up to the Republic of Ireland international squad was suitable reward. By the time of the World Cup Finals of 2002, Steve was an automatic choice for his country and he played in all four of the Republic's matches in the tournament.

In July 2003, Steve signed for Liverpool, initiating the next stage of an outstanding career. During the 2004–05 season he played in the Reds' League Cup final defeat to Chelsea at the Millennium Stadium. A bigger prize though was waiting for Steve – and the whole of the 'red side' of Merseyside – as Liverpool came back from 3–0 down to defeat AC Milan in the most dramatic Champions League final of all time.

Whatever their feelings for Rafael Benitez's side, there were plenty of Notts County supporters that felt a huge swell of pride as Steve Finnan, a former 'Pie, was crowned 'Champion of Europe'.

Eddie Gannon

Date of birth: 3 January 1921, Dublin
Died: 30 July 1989

Notts County record:

Appearances: League 107, FA Cup 11
Goals: League 2, FA Cup 0
Debut: 31 August 1946 v Bournemouth (h) won 1–0

Also played for: Hammond Lane, Distillery, Shelbourne, Sheffield Wednesday, Transport, Republic of Ireland (14 caps)
Managed: Shelbourne

Some say Eddie Gannon was one of the best players ever to represent Notts. A classy, stylish wing-half he had a great awareness on the pitch and was idolised by the supporters.

Eddie joined Notts immediately after the war, after initially making an impact with Irish club Shelbourne, where he had helped his side to two national titles and a cup final. With football enjoying large crowds as communities pulled together, they were exciting times at Meadow Lane as Notts experienced the 'Lawton era'. Tommy did not have top billing all to himself, as many felt that the 'tigerish' Gannon ensured the Magpies held midfield supremacy in most of their matches.

'Win it and give it' was Eddie's policy and his role in the side was vital. He was a strong, physical player with a good engine – he could run all day. All too rarely did he get within shooting distance of the opposition goal and he only recorded two strikes for Notts, both at home, against Bristol Rovers in November 1946 and against Port Vale the following October.

If his goalscoring was not attracting attention, his all-round play certainly was and plenty of other clubs were monitoring his steady development. His initial reward came by way of international recognition, with a call up to the full Republic of Ireland squad. Despite his association with a side occupying a mid-table place in Division Three South of the Football League, Eddie won his first cap against Switzerland in Dublin in December 1948. Although the Swiss won 1–0, Eddie impressed and it was inevitable that he was destined to play at a higher level.

For all their star names, Notts were unable to improve on their sixth place finish the previous year. The 1948–49 season did make the club's record books though. Having thumped Ipswich Town 9-2 and then Exeter City 9-0, Notts completed a hat-trick of huge home wins with an 11-1 mauling of Newport County. That result, on 15 January 1949, remains the Magpies' highest ever League victory. It also set the side up nicely for an FA Cup-tie against Liverpool at Anfield a fortnight later. Over 61,000 witnessed a plucky performance from 'Gannon and co' but they went down to a solitary second-half goal.

Shortly afterwards reality struck as the club sold Eddie to Sheffield Wednesday. There was something of an outcry from supporters but they knew the club could not refuse the £15,000 Wednesday were offering, a considerable sum at the time. It was also felt likely that Eddie would go on to savour top-flight football with the Owls: this he did, achieving promotion in his first full season, pipping near-neighbours Sheffield United on goal average by 0.008 of a goal!

Despite relegation the following season, Wednesday bounced back as Second Division champions in 1951–52. Having scored four goals from 204 League appearances over six years, Eddie returned home as Shelbourne's player-manager. He continued to represent his country until May 1955, when he won his 14th and final cap away against Germany, the World Champions.

Unhappy at not having total control over team selection, he left Shelbourne during the 1956–57 season and played out his career at fellow FAI League side Transport.

Eddie Gannon died in St James's Hospital, Dublin, in 1989, aged 68.

Alex Gibson

Date of birth: 28 November 1939, Kirkconnel, Ayrshire

Died: 22 November 2003

Notts County record:

Appearances: League 347, FA Cup 10, League Cup 16

Goals: League 10, FA Cup 0, League Cup 0

Debut: 7 September 1959 v Gateshead (a) drew 0–0

Also played for: Auchinleck, Boston United

Alex Gibson was still short of his 20th birthday when he was first drafted into the Notts County first team. The young centre-half had been acquired from Scottish junior football and proved to be an astute signing, going on to make 347 League appearances for the side, over a nine-year-period. A powerful, hard-tackling footballer, he provided yeoman service during a particularly unstable period in the club's history.

After making a couple of isolated appearances in the first team during September 1959, Alex had to wait until the New Year before enjoying a settled run in manager Frank Hill's side. His home debut, on 2 January against Crystal Palace, proved to be a turning point in the Magpies' fortunes. The South London team were swept aside 7–1, with Chris Joyce hitting a hat-trick. Notts went on to lose only two of their final 22 League matches to claim promotion and second place in the table, behind Walsall.

'Gibbo' made 17 appearances in his debut season, and 22 in the next, as Notts, with a young Tony Hateley finding the net with great regularity, posted a respectable fifth-place finish in Division Three.

Notts County's centenary season was 1962 and the footballing highlight was a special match on Wednesday 2 May between the club and an England XI preparing for the forthcoming World Cup in Chile. Although the national side won by three goals to one, Alex produced an exceptional performance, completely dominating his individual battle with Middlesbrough's Alan Peacock, the new England centre-forward.

Alex was an ever-present during the 1962–63 season but had to wait until the club had been relegated back to Division Four before netting his first goal for the club. It came from the penalty spot on 5 September 1964, away at Bradford Park Avenue – his 156th League match for the Magpies.

If goalscoring was not necessarily Alex's strongest suit, his reliability as a defender was unquestioned. With the whole-hearted respect of his colleagues, 'Gibbo' was a natural choice to succeed Gerry Carver as club skipper. His leadership qualities were essential as Notts slipped to the wrong end of Division Four and faced financial hardship and a threat to their continuing survival. Attendances plummeted at Meadow Lane and for a while the club feared the worst. The one remaining constant was Alex – a terrific servant and a true Notts County hero.

He played his final game for the club on 8 April 1969, an away draw at Workington. After leaving Notts, Alex joined Boston United, then a Northern Premier League side, under the stewardship of player-manager Jim Smith. For many years after ending his playing days, Alex was a popular figure working on a fruit market in Nottingham.

Alex Gibson died in 2003, just a few days short of his 64th birthday.

Mark Goodwin

Date of birth: 23 February 1960, Sheffield

Notts County record:

Appearances: League 237, FA Cup 15, League Cup 20, Others 10

Goals: League 23, FA Cup 0, League Cup 3, Others 0

Debut: 14 March 1981 v Grimsby Town (a) lost 1–2

Also played for: Leicester City, Walsall, Kettering Town, Eastwood Town, Arnold Town, Hucknall Town

All Notts County supporters will firmly believe that the club were always destined to win promotion from the old Division Two in 1981. Nevertheless, the acquisition of an experienced midfield battler for the final run-in helped ensure that the dream was fulfilled.

Despite being only 21 when he moved to Meadow Lane, Mark Goodwin had been in the Leicester City first team since he was 17 and had played in 91 League games for the Foxes. Additionally, he had got a medal to show for his efforts, having been part of the City side that had won the 1979–80 title.

His move to Notts mystified many, as he had been a regular in the First Division, but the £60,000 fee was agreeable to all parties. Having trodden the same path just a year earlier, Mark's obvious know-how was influential in the promotion drive and goals against Derby County and Watford came as an additional bonus.

Mark's arrival also coincided with the club reaching the Anglo-Scottish Cup final. Although he played in both legs against Chesterfield, the Magpies had loftier ambitions and did not do themselves justice as they let the opportunity of a trophy go amiss.

During Notts' first season back in Division One, Mark played in 38 of the 42 matches, scoring three times. He emerged as one of the club's most consistent performers during their three-year stay at that level, but showed considerable loyalty by remaining at Meadow Lane, even after the club had suffered successive relegations.

He said at the time, 'Notts made me a good offer to stay and, although I was hesitant at first, I felt I owed it to the club to give it a go.' Mark then added, 'There's a job to be done and we've all got to accept responsibility to try and get the club moving forward again.'

Individually, Mark could not have put in any more than he did during the next two campaigns. During that period he played in 88 League matches, scoring 10 goals from midfield, and maintained the very highest level of consistency.

In July 1987, after six years with Notts, he moved on to Walsall, with immediate success. In his first season with the Saddlers he helped them to promotion via the play-offs. Sadly, this was at the expense of his former club. Mark's first return to Meadow Lane in November 1987 had been an unhappy one, with Notts winning 3–1. Fortunes were reversed six months later as a similar scoreline helped Walsall through to the play-off final and an aggregate 4–2 victory.

The next two seasons did not go as well, with consecutive relegations, prompting Mark to call time on a League career that had totalled 420 matches. He joined Kettering before winding down his career as player-coach at some of Nottinghamshire's more prominent non-League clubs.

Rachid Harkouk

Date of birth: 19 May 1956, Chelsea

Notts County record:

Appearances: League 144, FA Cup 11, League Cup 12, Others 7

Goals: League 39, FA Cup 5, League Cup 5, Others 3

Debut: 2 August 1980 v Leyton Orient (h) drew 2–2 (Anglo-Scottish Cup)

Also played for: Crystal Palace, Queens Park Rangers

Whatever their nationality, Notts County fans found an additional side to follow during the 1986 World Cup Finals in Mexico. Their enigmatic midfielder Rachid Harkouk was a member of the Algerian squad and appeared in two matches during the tournament, against Northern Ireland and Spain. Sadly though, his selection had disastrous consequences for the player and for the club. Injured during the competition, he was unable to play competitive football again. His loss was a huge blow for County, with the 29-year-old still having much to offer. Nevertheless, he had already done enough to justify his place as a County legend.

Notts forked out just £50,000 for his talents, signing him from QPR, although Rachid had enjoyed a more successful period during a two-year stint at Crystal Palace. There, he had begun to attract attention for scoring some outrageous long-range thunderbolts, as well as bagging a couple of important winners against Brighton, the Eagles' deadly rivals.

Arriving at Meadow Lane in time for the start of the 1980–81 season he was seen as something of a loose cannon. Capable of blowing hot or cold, it seemed an unlikely choice of player for the Sirrel/Wilkinson combination to consider. As ever, though, their judgement was spot on. Rachid had experienced one or two disciplinary problems, on and off the pitch, while in London but he adapted quickly to the regime at County and his work rate was commendable.

A variety of nicknames accompanied the player, most noticeably 'Rash the Smash' and 'The Spider' and he proved easy to like, with a warm smile and mop of curly hair.

The Anglo-Scottish Cup enabled Rachid to make a goalscoring debut for the 'Pies and it proved to be a competition that he would enjoy. Notts advanced all the way to the final before losing to Chesterfield, with the Algerian playing his part by scoring in both legs of the semi-final against Kilmarnock.

In the League Rachid scored only four times, although he saved his best until last. Going to Stamford Bridge on 2 May 1981, Notts knew they would be promoted to the First Division if they won. Ironically, it was the man who was born in Chelsea who would emerge with star billing. Harkouk set up the first goal, scored for County by Trevor Christie, and then fired home a left-foot drive to seal the victory. Jubilant Magpies sang the name of 'Harkouk' all the way back up the M1!

A series of injuries disrupted Rachid's playing career but he would keep reappearing to score spectacular goals just when they were needed. In truth, there was not much for Notts to play for when Manchester United came to Meadow Lane on the last day of the 1982–83 season, although United needed a win to finish as League runners-up. Again Harkouk produced some stunning end-of-season finishing to upset the form book with a double and steer County to a famous 3–2 win.

In terms of goalscoring, his most prolific season came in 1984–85 when he hit 19 for Notts. His total included a hat-trick against Bolton Wanderers in the League cup. One year later he also hit three, this time against Scarborough in the FA Cup. That sort of form alerted the attentions of the Algerian selectors who decided to take him to Mexico with them.

After his enforced retirement Rachid remained in the Nottingham area, where he pursued a number of business interests.

Tony Hateley

Date of birth: 13 June 1941, Derby

Notts County record:

Appearances: League 188, FA Cup 13, League Cup 6
Goals: League 109, FA Cup 4, League Cup 1
Debut: 8 November 1958 v Stockport County (a) drew 1–1

Also played for: Aston Villa, Chelsea, Liverpool, Coventry City, Birmingham City, Oldham Athletic, Bromsgrove Rovers, Prescot

'I'd be worth a fortune nowadays', reflects Tony Hateley, modestly surveying a return of 109 goals from his 188 League games for Notts. 'Whenever Les Bradd reminds me that he broke my record I have to point out that it took him three times as long!'

Tony was, quite simply, a brilliant goalscorer but fate played its part in him becoming a striker. 'I was a young centre-half, keen to make an impression. During Tuesday training we would play first team against the rest. A couple of forwards were out injured so Tim Coleman told me to have a go up front. I scored a couple and must have impressed because they tried me there for the reserves. We went to Shrewsbury and I managed to score five!'

A first-team debut beckoned at the tender age of 17. 'It was away against Stockport – I had a shocker but still managed to score, though I can't remember it at all.' A run of 10 matches at the end of the 1959–60 season brought eight goals – enough to guarantee a starting berth the following season. Apart from managing to net a few, Tony's contribution had helped Notts clinch second place in the table and promotion to the Third Division.

In September 1960, Tony scored his first senior hat-trick at home to Barnsley. It would be the first of six he would bag for the Magpies. His haul that season was 27 goals, followed by 21 in 1961–62 and 22 the year after. Wonderfully consistent, Tony's height made him the 'king of the skies' as he soared time after time to bullet headers home. Not since Tommy Lawton had County fans been able to worship a striker who possessed the same aerial threat.

Tony Cooper from Tamworth, a 'Pie for more than 50 years, sums up exactly what Tony meant to Notts. 'To me he was the most exciting striker the club have ever had. It was the excitement generated at set pieces that I remember most vividly, as it seemed there was always a better than average chance of Tony outjumping the defence and smashing a header past a helpless keeper.'

During the 1962 centenary season Notts played host to an England XI. Although the national team won 3–1, Tony grabbed the goal for the hosts. His stock was rising and with the sheer volume of goals, scouts were flocking to see him. Eventually it was time to move on – Aston Villa's bid of £20,000 being sufficient to secure his signature. Those that mourned his departure were eventually rewarded when, after a lengthy period of success in the top flight, Tony came 'home'. 'I was delighted to return to Notts', he says. 'Under Jimmy Sirrel it was an exciting period and I thoroughly enjoyed being part of another promotion-winning side.'

The 1971–72 season saw Tony notch his 100th League goal for Notts and he had added another nine before Chesterfield came to Meadow Lane in March. 'A big defender fell right across my right knee and that was it – my inside medial ligament had gone. I was operated on and later played a few games for Oldham but that challenge effectively ended my career.'

Tony spent a couple of years setting up and running a catalogue business before accepting an offer to join Everton as their Lottery Manager. After four years at Goodison, Tony became the Liverpool area rep for Thwaites Brewery.

Aside from his normal working week, Tony has been actively involved in fund-raising for the SPARKS children's charity. 'For 25 years we've been holding golf events and have raised something like £9 million in that time.'

Through the 1980s and 1990s the Hateley name remained prominent, with son Mark gaining 32 caps for England. 'I enjoyed watching him play at places like Milan, Monaco and Rangers', says Tony. 'But for all that I enjoyed my time, particularly at Notts, and I'd love the fans to know how much I appreciated their warmth and best wishes during both my spells with the club.'

Paul Heffernan

Date of birth: 29 December 1981, Dublin

Notts County record:

Appearances: League 100, FA Cup 4, League Cup 5, Others 5

Goals: League 35, FA Cup 1, League Cup 1, Others 0

Debut: 20 April 2000 v Oldham Athletic (h) lost 0–1

Also played for: Newtown, Bristol City, Doncaster Rovers

Paul Heffernan was like a breath of fresh air to Notts' fans. The young Dubliner burst onto the first-team scene towards the end of the 1999–2000 season and immediately impressed with his eagerness and enthusiasm.

As back-up striker to Mark Stallard and Danny Allsopp, young 'Heff' had to bide his time and learn his craft, but began to really establish himself in the side in the 2001–02 season.

His first goal for the club salvaged a point at the JJB Stadium in a 1–1 draw against Wigan Athletic, a moment Paul will never forget. 'It was my first start for the club. Darren Caskey floated a free-kick in and somehow I got in amongst all the bodies and managed to head it in at the far post.'

During a relatively brief career at Meadow Lane, Paul blasted his way into the record books with a four-goal haul. His 'day to remember' came on 21 February 2004, playing against Stockport County at Meadow Lane. Scoring all the goals in Notts' 4–1 victory, Paul became the first Magpie to achieve the feat since Jimmy Jackson hit four against West Ham United on New Year's Day in 1955. Heff's haul began as early as the second minute. Another before the break, a penalty for the hat-trick and a fourth near the end completed the tally. 'To be honest, it was just one of those days', he reflects. 'None of the goals were really spectacular but I had another couple of decent chances as well, so might have scored five or six!'

The feat came during a great run of form in home matches. At Meadow Lane between 9 November and 2 March, Paul scored 12 goals in just eight games. That period also included another hat-trick, his first in League football. 'QPR were on a great run of form when they came to us on Boxing Day. I stuck away a penalty to put us 3–2 up but they scored a last-minute equaliser. Although I'd scored all the goals the result took a bit of the gloss off the achievement.'

Paul's tally for the 2003–04 season was 21, putting him comfortably ahead as the club's top scorer. Amongst his better memories of a fantastic individual campaign are from a game in which he did not score and that resulted in a Notts defeat. 'The League Cup match against Chelsea at Stamford Bridge was just amazing. Abramovich's millions against a club with absolutely nothing and we fought and fought until the end. We really acquitted ourselves well and were always in with a shout.'

Paul's favourite Magpies goal came at Meadow Lane against Bristol City. 'I flicked it over a couple of players and then hit a cracking left-footed volley past the 'keeper.' Somewhat ironically, Paul joined up with the Bristol club when he left Notts in the summer of 2004 but will always remember his days with County, especially when he pops back to see the folks in Ireland. 'The two match-balls I scored the hat-tricks with are all autographed and proudly on display there. Definite reminders of some very happy times!'

Prior to the start of the 2005–06 season Paul was on the move again, transferring to Doncaster Rovers for a fee of £125,000.

Ian Hendon

Date of birth: 5 December 1971, Ilford, Essex

Notts County record:

Appearances: League 83, FA Cup 9, League Cup 5, Others 0
Goals: League 6, FA Cup 0, League Cup 1, Others 0
Debut: 25 February 1997 v Millwall (a) lost 0–1

Also played for: Tottenham Hotspur, Portsmouth, Leyton Orient, Barnsley, Birmingham City, Northampton Town, Sheffield Wednesday, Peterborough, Barnet

Ian Hendon was captain of Notts County's Division Three championship triumph in 1997–98, although he admits he was fortunate to wear the armband. 'Gary Strodder was sent off in a pre-season County Cup match against Nottingham Forest and Sam Allardyce, the manager, punished him by taking the captaincy away. I do a lot of shouting on the pitch anyway, so I think Sam thought I'd be ideal to do it.' Whether the decision was influenced by sentimentality is unclear but Sam obviously rated 'Hendo', making him his first signing after taking over at Notts.

Ian arrived at Meadow Lane in early 1997 after graduating through the youth ranks at Tottenham and then cutting his professional teeth during a spell of over three years at Leyton Orient. His arrival at Meadow Lane was timely. The club was nose-diving into the bottom division and morale was not high. The new manager had his work cut out but, says Ian, it was clear he was going to succeed. 'Sam got everyone organised. Immediately there was a belief that we were going to bounce straight back up. As an ex-defender himself he soon sorted out the back four. We worked hard on set-play routines and became a difficult side to score against.'

Notts romped to the title, winning it by 28 March, the earliest date any domestic title has been clinched. Several club records were also established: 10 consecutive League wins; 15 away victories throughout the season, including seven in succession; and only five defeats, the fewest ever.

With the championship already claimed, it was time for Ian to undergo some long-needed treatment. 'Both Ian Richardson and myself had struggled with hernia problems for several months. As soon as the title was guaranteed we both went in for the operation and began rehab in time for the new season. It was disappointing to miss the final run-in but still an honour to be around to lift the trophy as captain.'

Notts' championship-winning side contained several players who moved on to play at a higher level, notably Steve Finnan. 'He deserves all the success he's had', says Ian. 'Finns is so dedicated, the total professional. When we were at Notts he played just in front of me, on the right. For looking after him so well I still reckon he owes me some of his wages!'

Ian scored just a handful of goals during his time with the Magpies but has a clear favourite. 'I hit a free-kick against Macclesfield that flew in from about 25 yards. The 'keeper was about 6ft 4in but he couldn't get near it as it went straight into the top corner.'

He also recalls being handed the responsibility of taking penalties. 'When Gary Jones left I took over and one of the first was against Millwall. Nigel Spink was in goal and I remember thinking "I used to watch this guy on television as a kid". It probably wasn't the right approach but fortunately I scored!'

After just two years with Notts, Ian moved on, playing for a succession of clubs and taking his career first-team appearances total beyond the 600 mark. There was more success for Ian at the end of the 2004–05 campaign as he held aloft the Conference trophy, after skippering Barnet's successful push for a return to the Football League. He feels the season mirrored his title triumph at Notts. 'On both occasions we were the best side by miles and deserved the title. Barnet played consistently well and were fortunate that we had a natural goalscorer like Guiliano Grazioli to accept most of the chances. Gary Jones did the same at Notts.'

As full-backs go, Ian Hendon was as dependable as they come. A consistently high performer, he was tough in the tackle and a captain to rely upon – so obviously proud to lead the Magpies to success.

Paul Hooks

Date of birth: 30 May 1959, Wallsend, Tyne and Wear

Notts County record:

Appearances: League 173, FA Cup 9, League Cup 15, Others 19

Goals: League 30, FA Cup 1, League Cup 6, Others 4

Debut: 14 May 1977 v Charlton Athletic (h) lost 0–1

Also played for: Derby County, Boston United, Cotgrave Miners Welfare

Paul Hooks was an integral part of the Notts County side that won promotion to the top flight in May 1981. Having graduated through the youth ranks as a striker, he went on to prove his versatility by later switching to midfield.

He went on to play over 200 times for the Magpies and was always capable of bagging a crucial goal on a big occasion. The fans took a particular liking to him, as twice he netted against Nottingham Forest in League matches, a statistic that he was undeniably proud of!

Born in the North East, he moved down to Ollerton, a Nottinghamshire mining village as a youngster and was overjoyed when he was given an apprenticeship at Meadow Lane. His first-team debut arrived at the end of the 1976–77 season when, as a 17-year-old, he was included for a home match against Charlton Athletic.

Working hard through the summer months, he signed a professional contract and put himself in the frame for regular first-team inclusion. His cause was helped when he netted a debut goal for the club in a real see-saw match in the Anglo-Scottish Cup against Sheffield United – Notts eventually winning 5–4.

Ronnie Fenton, the County manager, put young Paul on the bench for the opening match of the season against Blackburn Rovers but could not have envisaged what would happen when he brought him on for Martyn Busby. Within three minutes Paul was sent off for a challenge on a defender! Many inexperienced players have crumbled under such a start to their professional careers but Paul blossomed, especially after Jimmy Sirrel returned into the manager's hot seat.

In the never-to-be-forgotten season of 1980–81 it was Paul Hooks that ensured a winning start with the opening-day decider against Bolton Wanderers. That was the first of five League goals that season, usually playing from a wide position where he could get forward to support Trevor Christie or help out in midfield when needed.

County's promotion enabled Paul to have his first taste of the top flight and from the first match, a 1–0 win over Aston Villa, he looked comfortable at the higher level. When the Magpies crossed the Trent on 23 January 1982, it was Paul who scored the first goal of the match as Notts defeated their closest rivals 2–0, a very sweet victory indeed! In December of the same year, he completed a personal double over the Reds by scoring Notts' second in the 3–2 home victory.

Three months later, in March 1983, Paul was on his way out of Meadow Lane, when a bid of £50,000 took him to Derby County, who were then in Division Two. Over the next two seasons he scored four times in 59 League appearances for the Baseball Ground side but following their relegation he was released at the end of the 1984–85 season.

After a brief trial at Mansfield Town, Paul moved into the non-League game, joining Boston United for a couple of years before signing for Cotgrave Miners Welfare.

David Hunt

Date of birth: 17 April 1959, Leicester

Notts County record:

Appearances: League 336, FA Cup 22, League Cup 28, Others 21

Goals: League 28, FA Cup 2, League Cup 5, Others 2

Debut: 17 March 1978 v Charlton Athletic (a) drew 0–0

Also played for: Derby County, Aston Villa, Mansfield Town

David Hunt was a key member of the Notts midfield for nine years and an ever-present in Jimmy Sirrel's side that won promotion back to the top flight in 1981.

Signing for a new club is always a special moment in the career of any footballer. For David, it was an insight into things to come. 'I was mainly being used as a sub at Derby County when I heard of County's interest. I spoke to the manager and Jimmy said he'd take me to speak to the chairman. Before I knew it, I was on a train heading towards London. We went into the buffet car and ordered fish and chips. Jimmy squirted tomato ketchup all over his, then licked the top of the bottle – I had to decline when he offered it to me, "David can I interest you?" '

On arrival in the capital, David was taken to the Houses of Parliament to meet the Chairman, Jack Dunnett MP. 'We talked and agreed contracts and eventually got hold of Tommy Docherty, my manager at Derby. With just three minutes to go before the end of the transfer deadline, the deal was done.' Despite the unique location of the signing, there was one more surprise in store for David that day. 'Jimmy shook my hand and said, "Cheerio, I'll see you in Nottingham." I was left to make my own way home!'

David immediately cemented a place in the County first team but had to wait a while before he got on the scoresheet, though it's overdue arrival was extremely timely. 'My first Notts goal is probably the most memorable I scored for the club. It was the winner in a 4–3 thriller away at Blackburn. The ball broke nicely to me off a defender and I just curled it into the bottom corner.'

Full of energy and passion, David Hunt worked tirelessly for the side and underestimated his own value. 'My role was just to win the ball and give it to Don Masson.' The supporters knew that he was worth much more than that when he was presented with the club's Player of the Year award for season 1979–80.

While individual accolades are welcome, footballers delight in team successes and the promotion season of 1980–81 was particularly satisfying for David. Along with Tristan Benjamin and Brian Kilcline, he was one of three ever-presents in the 'Pies line-up. 'We worked hard for our success and thoroughly deserved it', he says. 'We were well-organised, we got results and we believed in ourselves.'

David still smiles at the memory of winning promotion to the top flight. 'When the whistle went and we'd beaten Chelsea 2–0, I could see how much it meant to everyone – it was a very special moment.'

Never the most prolific of goalscorers David can boast of netting a League hat-trick for Notts. 'It was at home against Bristol City in 1985. Everything went right for me that day – I've still got the ball on display at home!'

After leaving Meadow Lane, David played for both Aston Villa and Mansfield Town before setting up his own soccer school in Ashby-de-la-Zouch. Working with youngsters every day clearly gives him immense pleasure. 'We are actively involved in the community in providing football coaching for all ages from 5 to 16. Although we run it as a commercial venture it means more to me to see youngsters enjoying their football.'

Albert Iremonger

Date of birth: 15 June 1884, Wilford, Notts
Died: 9 March 1958

Notts County record:
Appearances: League 564, FA Cup 37
Debut: 1 April 1905 v Sheffield Wednesday (a) lost 0–1

Also played for: Jardines Athletic, Lincoln City

Larger-than-life and twice as eccentric, there was only one Albert Iremonger! While Notts County are very proud of the succession of high-quality goalkeepers that have served them over the years, none have come close to matching Albert's appearance tally for the club.

Towering over his contemporaries, both in stature and ability, Albert was the custodian of the Notts goal for over 20 years and played in a record number of matches for the club. At 6ft 5in, Albert was a giant of a man who went on to become the club's longest-serving goalkeeper. Many felt he was the best in the land in his position but England caps eluded him, probably due to his character and temperament rather than his goalkeeping skills.

When riled by opposition, teammates or officialdom he was prone to wandering out of his area to discuss the matter further. On several occasions the matter of disciplining their star attraction was brought to the attention of the Board of Directors.

It is believed that much of the Iremonger myth is pure fabrication, though he was notorious for his arguments. On any number of occasions he brought embarrassment upon the club – he was undoubtedly a loose cannon.

While there were many calls to dispense with Albert's services, the club knew they had the best goalkeeper in the land and one who served them, with great distinction, either side of the Great War.

The young Albert grew up in Wilford and played his football for a local team, Jardines Athletic. He was also an outstanding cricketer and played for the county side on a number of occasions. His brother Jimmy was an equally adept sportsman, playing cricket for Nottinghamshire and at full-back for Forest. In later years Jimmy also served as County's trainer.

Albert was taken on by Notts after an impressive series of trial outings. While his physical appearance may have been startling, his goalkeeping could not be faulted. Once in the County team, he was there to stay. Between February 1907 and October 1912, Albert played in 211 consecutive League matches, a run that surely will never be broken. Typically, it was suspension through ill discipline, rather than an injury, which broke his sequence. Back in the side, Albert then continued his appearance tally right up until the outbreak of war. He 'guested' for Notts on many occasions and resumed his career when League football restarted.

In his two-decade association with the club, Albert experienced three relegations and two promotions and was part of the side that made the transition from Trent Bridge to Meadow Lane. He toured both Denmark and Spain as Notts embarked on their first overseas adventures and played in the 1922 FA Cup semi-final defeat to Huddersfield Town, the last occasion in which the Magpies reached the last four.

Regrettably, though, the national selectors continually overlooked him, although he did play in a trial match and also made appearances for the Football League representative side.

In 1926, Albert signed for Lincoln City, where he played for one final season. He had played in 564 League games for Notts, keeping 183 clean sheets.

After retirement, Albert Iremonger became a licensee, returning to Wilford to run the Ferry Inn. He died in 1958, aged 73.

Michael Johnson

Date of birth: 4 July 1973, Nottingham

Notts County record:
Appearances: League 107, FA Cup 4, League Cup 9, Others 15
Goals: League 0, FA Cup 0, League Cup 0, Others 1
Debut: 22 October 1991 v Sheffield United (a) drew 3–3 (Zenith Data Systems Cup)

Also played for: Birmingham City, Derby County, Jamaica (14 caps)

Penalty shoot-outs have featured quite prominently in the career of Michael Johnson and that is how his Notts County debut started. 'My first match was in the ZDS Cup and we ended up losing on penalties against Sheffield United. I thought I'd had quite a decent game but I was far too nervous to take one of the spot-kicks.'

At just 18 years of age, the young defender had impressed enough to warrant a start in the next League match – away at Arsenal. 'I'll never forget that match and I felt so proud to be playing in front of a full house at Highbury. I played in the centre of defence with Dean Yates but he had to go off injured, so in the second half I had Gary Lund alongside me!'

'Johnno's' links with Notts began when he was just 14. 'I was playing for Nottingham Schoolboys on the astroturf on Wilford Lane. Mick Walker was watching and afterwards he invited me to come to the club and talk about being taken on.'

Although Michael has often stood in at full-back, he knew from an early age that if he was to make it in the professional game it would be in the heart of the defence. 'Fortunately I've always been fairly quick and been able to read the game pretty well. For someone who's not the tallest I've got a fairly decent spring as well!'

The highlights of his time with the Magpies are obvious – two Wembley appearances and a 1994 win over the local rivals. 'The day we beat Forest at home was just unbelievable. The whole city was buzzing before the game and then, lo and behold, it was Charlie Palmer who scored the winner. He wasn't the most renowned of goalscorers but he knew how to celebrate. I think he ran the length of Nottingham when it went in!'

Sadly for Michael he never did get to experience the same thrill as a County player. 'I never did manage to score a goal for Notts. I hit the post a couple of times, particularly late on at Wembley against Brescia.'

Notts' Anglo-Italian adventures have been much-maligned by some people but certainly not by the players. 'I thoroughly enjoyed the matches', says Michael. 'It was a great thrill to play against people like Romania's Hagi and Thomas Skuhravy, the Czech striker, and I still treasure my winners' medal.'

In September 1995, Michael was transferred to Birmingham City after making more than 100 League appearances for the Magpies. 'I didn't really want to leave but the club had been relegated, Barry Fry was interested in signing me and Notts decided they were happy to let me go.'

During his time with the Blues, Michael was reacquainted with more penalty shoot-outs than he would care to remember. He ended up a loser in a play-off semi-final and a League Cup final shoot-out, yet won promotion to the Premiership after beating Norwich City by the same method. His goal drought was also broken with a total of 17 goals for the St Andrews' club.

Michael's big-match temperament attracted attention with several international call-ups for Jamaica. 'Both my mother and father came from there and it was such a great thrill to pull on the shirt and play for them. It was really an emotional thing for me to line up for the national anthem in front of a packed stadium.'

The 'Reggae Boy' moved on to Derby County for the 2003–04 season and suffered more play-off disappointment with a semi-final defeat a year later.

Although everyone usually refers to him as 'Johnno', Michael admits there is one other nickname that he is really proud of. 'Occasionally, at all my clubs, when things have gone well the fans have chanted "Magic, Magic, Johnson". As he was one of the great sports stars of all time it makes me feel very honoured to hear it.'

The word 'magic' is fairly appropriate to sum up Michael's career, as he reveals. 'Football has been so good to me. I've managed to achieve just about everything I ever set out to do and it is thanks to Notts County that I was given that opportunity.'

Tommy Johnson

Date of birth: 15 January 1971, Newcastle

Notts County record:

Appearances: League 118, FA Cup 5, League Cup 9, Others 17

Goals: League 47, FA Cup 1, League Cup 5, Others 4

Debut: 24 September 1988 v Preston North End (h) drew 0–0

Also played for: Derby County, Aston Villa, Celtic, Everton, Sheffield Wednesday, Kilmarnock, Gillingham, Sheffield United, Scunthorpe United

No matter how well a side plays, somebody has to stick the ball in the back of the net. Notts County were fortunate in that, on two of the biggest days in their history, they had Tommy Johnson. 'TJ' scored the opener against Tranmere Rovers in the 1990 play-off final and a year later broke the hearts of the Brighton supporters with a couple of well-taken goals to ensure a second consecutive promotion.

County's scout in the North East must take immense credit for getting Tommy to Meadow Lane. 'John Allan watched me play so many times and he badly wanted me to go to Nottingham and have a look. My family weren't so keen – they hoped I'd play for Newcastle United. Anyway, I went and was so impressed because everybody made me feel really welcome. I was still only about 14 or 15 and I was able to go down in the school holidays and train with the first team. Mick Walker did a lot of the training sessions then and he was really helpful towards me.'

It was not too long before a professional contract was signed and at just 17 years of age Tommy was given his senior debut, coming off the bench in a League match against Preston. His first two senior goals came in a 3–0 win over Huddersfield Town. 'They are probably still the most memorable of my career because they were the first. My mate Mark Draper scored the other goal, to make it even more special.'

Neil Warnock's arrival at Notts galvanised the club and helped foster a terrific team spirit. 'All of the lads seemed to get on well and have kept in touch with each other over the years.'

In just his second season with the Magpies, Tommy finished as the leading goalscorer, netting 18 in the League and another couple in the play-offs, including his goal at Wembley. 'Kevin Bartlett did well to pull the ball back from the right. I just turned and hit it left-footed and remember it being an unbelievable feeling when it went in.'

That goal set Notts on their way to a 2–0 victory over Tranmere. One year later it was a case of *déjà vu*, with the chance of a further promotion. This time the flame-haired striker netted twice, one a real collectors' item. 'I still can't believe I scored a goal at Wembley with my head. To be fair, it was a brilliant cross from Phil Turner and it just flicked off the wig!' His second goal was a real stunner, a low drive into the far corner after good work by Dave Regis.

Earlier that season 'TJ' had scored his first senior hat-trick, at home to Blackburn Rovers. It was to be the only one he would score for the Magpies before leaving to join Derby County in March 1992 for a fee of £1.3 million. Subsequent high-profile moves followed to both Aston Villa and Celtic before Tommy joined the 'free transfer brigade' and moved clubs more frequently in search of regular football.

He looked to have wound down his playing career when he accepted a coaching position at Sheffield United, under his old mentor Neil Warnock, but in the summer of 2005 he moved again. 'Everyone keeps telling me to play as long as I can, so when Brian Laws offered me the chance to continue my career at Scunthorpe United I thought, "Why not?" '

Tom Johnston

Date of birth: 30 December 1918, Berwick-on-Tweed

Died: 27 November 1994

Notts County record:

Appearances: League 267, FA Cup 18

Goals: League 88, FA Cup 4

Debut: 21 August 1948 v Torquay United (a) lost 1–3

Also played for: Hearts, Peterborough United, Northampton Town, Leicester City, Nottingham Forest

Managed: Heanor Town, Rotherham United, Grimsby Town, Huddersfield Town, York City

It is perhaps understandable, though a little unfortunate, that Tom Johnston's career as a Magpie tends to be overlooked a little. He was, quite simply, a wonderful footballer with a venomous shot and an instinct for seizing on the half-chance. Tom's only crime, if it can be classed as such, was to play in the same Notts County team as the household names of Lawton and Sewell. Nevertheless, Tom played more matches for Notts than either of his illustrious teammates and his tally of 88 League goals still finds him sitting high on the club's table of all-time scorers.

After the war, Tom crossed the Trent, signing from Nottingham Forest and enjoying a magnificent debut season in 1948–49. Supporters have never fully understood how County could finish only 11th in Division Three (South), with Sewell, Lawton and Johnston knocking in 70 League goals between them – Tom's share of which was 24.

Despite the collective failure, Tom did enjoy some individual highlights. In consecutive matches, against Crystal Palace and Watford in February 1949, he completed the unusual statistic of recording a hat-trick in each. He added another couple of goals on the day County demolished Newport County 11–1 to record their highest-ever winning margin and was part of the side that bravely went out of the FA Cup at Liverpool in front of 61,000 fans.

The disappointment of the previous campaign was soon forgotten as Notts did win the championship during the 1950–51 season. Playing wide on the left, Tom contributed another 15 goals to the cause, as well as setting up countless others. Back in Division Two for the first time since 1935, Notts just about kept their heads above water, with a 17th place finish. Again, Tom Johnston should take a large chunk of the credit because he contributed 14 goals in the League, making him joint top-scorer alongside Jackie Sewell.

A couple of less productive seasons followed, largely because Tom was being employed in a much deeper role, but during the 1953–54 season, long after the departure of the 'big two', Tom was switched to centre-forward with great success. He was easily the club's top scorer, hitting 16 from 38 starts. He finished his time at Meadow Lane by moving into the half-back line and he made his final appearance for the club in December 1956 at home to Grimsby Town.

Keen to remain in the game, Tom turned to coaching, moving initially to Birmingham City before landing his first League manager's position at Rotherham United. He gave valued service wherever he went, spending four years with the Millers, two at Grimsby Town and then lengthy spells at Huddersfield Town and York City, with whom he won promotion from the Third Division in 1974. He then returned to Huddersfield for a second stint from 1975 to 1978.

Tom then retired back to Stapleford, Notts, where he sadly passed away in 1994.

Barrie Jones

Date of birth: 31 October 1938, Barnsley

Notts County record:

Appearances: League 42, FA Cup 2, League Cup 6
Goals: League 15, FA Cup 0, League Cup 2
Debut: 28 March 1962 v Shrewsbury Town (a) lost 0–3

Also played for: Kings Lynn

It is always a special occasion for a player when he makes his home debut – a first opportunity for the fans to cast a critical eye over a recent signing, or a promising youngster who has been promoted from the reserves.

Barrie Jones' first appearance at Meadow Lane for the Magpies could not have gone much better. In fact, within the time it takes to say 'Who's the new number nine?' Barrie had achieved a feat which was to put him in the *Guinness Book of Records* as scorer of the joint-second fastest goal of all time. It was an impressive start for the ex-soldier, who was bought out of the Army to supplement Notts' attacking options, which already included the likes of skipper Bob Forrest, youngsters Tony Hateley and Jeff Astle and the more experienced Peter Bircumshaw.

Barrie had played in some far-flung places, including Tripoli, while serving his country, but his potential as a professional footballer was clear for all to see. Possessing plenty of pace, an assured touch and a keen eye for goal, he was seen as a decent acquisition by the Magpies.

His first match did not go well – the team were awful and went down 3–0 away at Shrewsbury. Match number two was played at Meadow Lane on 31 March 1962, with Torquay United providing the opposition.

Barrie lives with his wife, Angela, in retirement in Kirkby-in-Ashfield, Nottinghamshire. Sadly, in September 2002, he suffered a stroke which left him with his speech impaired. Son Steven, though, is able to recall how Barrie entered the history books, with a goal scored just six seconds after the kick-off.

'Dad told me many times about how the goal happened. He'd kicked the match off, tapping the ball to a teammate, although he's never been sure who it was. He then set off, running diagonally to the right, towards the centre of the 18-yard box. Bob Forrest had received the ball by now and he rolled it perfectly into dad's path.'

The Torquay goalkeeper could not have expected to be involved so early in the game but he reacted quickly, as Steven reveals. 'The 'keeper was out to the edge of his box but dad hit it under him with his first touch, helping the ball on from the direction of Bob's pass. Both players collided and my dad needed a couple of minutes treatment for an injury to his left knee before he could continue.'

Notts went on to win the match 2–0 and afterwards the referee confirmed that he had timed the goal at exactly six seconds on his stopwatch. After such an amazing introduction to his time as a Notts County player, everything else Barrie achieved at the club would always be classed as 'after the Lord Mayor's Show'. However, he did claim a respectable strike rate of 15 goals from his 42 League appearances.

Between 20 September and 6 October 1962, Barrie enjoyed a hot streak in front of goal, netting in five consecutive matches. With the competition for striking places at its most fierce, Barrie often had to bide his time for a regular run in the first team.

During the 1962–63 season, Notts abandoned the famous stripes and wore a plain white shirt, with black trim. Although there was a slight improvement in the League position, the club reverted to their more familiar colours the next season. Unfortunately, the Magpies' fortunes plummeted during the 1963–64 campaign, finishing bottom of Division Three. There were significant changes to the playing staff and Barrie left to join Kings Lynn just over two years after moving to Meadow Lane. His six-second strike remains the quickest ever scored by a Notts player, a record likely to stand for all time.

Tom Keetley

Date of birth: 16 November 1898, Normanton, Derbyshire

Died: 19 August 1958

Notts County record:

Appearances: League 103, FA Cup 7

Goals: League 94, FA Cup 4

Debut: 31 August 1929 v Bristol City (h) won 3–1

Also played for: Victoria Ironworks, Bradford Park Avenue, Doncaster Rovers, Lincoln City

The 1930s began with Notts County possessing one of the most prolific strikers in the country. Tom Keetley had been scoring goals for fun at Doncaster Rovers, notching 185 in just 241 League and cup matches between 1923 and 1929 for the Belle Vue club.

One of 12 brothers, four of whom played for Doncaster, Tom was a goal machine. During the 1928–29 season he smashed in 40 goals, including six against Ashington in a 7–4 thrashing. Little wonder then that Rovers were distraught when Tom revealed plans to set up a business in Derby. They did not want to lose him but refused his request just to turn up on matchdays. Quite literally, the hitman was on Notts County's doorstep looking for a club. What a stroke of luck!

Stepping up a division was never likely to be a problem for someone who thrived on his speed of thought inside the penalty area. He sounded an ominous warning to any would-be doubters by blasting a hat-trick on his County debut. Injury disrupted his first full season at Meadow Lane and he only scored a dozen goals from 20 starts. The following year though, undoubtedly belonged to Tom.

Leaving the remainder of Division Three South in their wake – runners-up Crystal Palace finished eight points adrift – Notts won the championship helped by an immense contribution from Keetley. An amazing 39 League goals from 34 matches, plus another two in the FA Cup, gave the striker the best return ever recorded in a single season by a County player. Amongst his haul in that particular campaign were four trebles and a four-goal tally in a 6–1 home rout against Fulham. Notts managed to score in every single home fixture that season.

Tom Keetley's goal-per-game ratio of 94 League goals from just 103 matches for Notts stands comparison with anyone. When he was hot, he was very hot. Short, stocky and with a lethal shot, Tom tended to score his goals in clusters, as his collection of 10 hat-tricks for the Magpies would testify, a club record.

During the 1931–32 season Keetley achieved a feat never equalled by any Football League player. He scored hat-tricks in consecutive away matches – against Plymouth Argyle, Manchester United and Chesterfield.

After leaving Notts he played 10 games for Lincoln City before announcing his retirement from the game. He had scored a total of 284 League goals during his career, from just 330 appearances.

The legendary goal-poacher later became a licensee, running the Rose and Crown Hotel at Chellaston, Derbyshire. He passed away in 1958, aged 59.

Brian Kilcline

Date of birth: 7 May 1962, Nottingham

Notts County record:

Appearances: League 158, FA Cup 10, League Cup 15, Others 9
Goals: League 9, FA Cup 2, League Cup 1, Others 1
Debut: 5 September 1979 v Torquay United (a) won 1–0 (League Cup)

Also played for: Coventry City, Oldham Athletic, Newcastle United, Swindon Town, Mansfield Town, Halifax Town, Altrincham, England Under-21 (3 caps)

Notts County broke the mould when they introduced Brian Kilcline into their first team, as he explains. 'We'd become known as a side who only included big, left-footed defenders. I was big but only used my left for standing on!' He was not even a defender when he sprang to prominence in the County FA sides. 'I played up front and broke some scoring records when I was young but couldn't do it once I'd been taken on by Notts.'

Brian recalls the day his conversion to a defender began. 'I was playing for the reserves against Stoke City when I was put back to centre-half. Someone, I think it was Colin Murphy, urged me to "try kicking them instead of letting them kick you". I marked Lee Chapman that day and actually enjoyed getting stuck in.'

The big defender soon acquired the nickname of 'Killer' as his first-team breakthrough developed. He made 16 appearances in the 1979–80 season, scoring his first goal on the final day in a 3–3 draw against Birmingham City. 'I can't even remember it', he confesses. 'All I recall is that it put us 3–2 up and really frightened them because they needed at least a draw to secure promotion. They did manage to equalise before the end though.'

If that match ended in jubilation for the St Andrews side, a year on it was Notts' turn. While many of his teammates recall the excitement of winning promotion, Brian reflects on the stupidest tannoy announcement he'd ever heard. 'When we went 2–0 up at Chelsea there was a pitch invasion from their "so-called" fans. We were taken back to the dressing room but I heard the man on the PA system say, "If you don't get off the pitch, the match will be abandoned." That was what they wanted, so even more ran on!' Eventually the police did restore order and the Magpies secured their historic return to the top flight. Brian had more than played his part by appearing in every single match during that momentous season.

Those that felt that County would be ill-equipped for life in Division One had reckoned without a steely spirit and a determination to do well. 'Football really is all about trying to prove people wrong. We were well prepared, very organised and totally professional.' It was that sort of attitude that saw Notts record an opening day victory at Aston Villa and come back from a goal down to beat Arsenal, with Brian getting the last-minute winner.

His performances were getting noticed and international recognition came with the first of three England Under-21 selections. During County's three-season stay in the top division, Brian played in exactly 100 League matches but, following their relegation in 1984, he was allowed to join Coventry City for a fee of £60,000. 'There comes a time when you are ready for a new challenge. I'd been at Meadow Lane since I was 16 and needed to try something new.'

Brian could not have envisaged how the next phase of his career would pan out. For the first time in their history, with Brian as captain, Coventry went to Wembley and won the 1987 FA Cup final by beating Spurs 3–2.

Between 1991 and 1998, Brian changed clubs on five occasions before bringing down the curtain on a career which had totalled over 500 first-team appearances. Settling down in West Yorkshire, Brian moved into property redevelopment – while also fulfilling an ambition to travel. 'My wife Lynn and I have been fairly successful in the property market over the years and we rent out accommodation which enables us to go abroad fairly frequently. Don't imagine we stay in five-star hotels though – we take our backpacks and rough it. That's something we both enjoy very much.'

Brian also maintains a watchful eye on the game, as a football reporter for the Press Association. He does not get to see the Magpies that often but remains grateful for the start they gave him. 'I enjoyed my time at Notts and I'll always be thankful that they helped set me up to lead the life I have.'

Tommy Lawton

Date of birth: 6 October 1919, Bolton, Lancashire
Died: 6 November 1996

Notts County record:

Appearances: League 151, FA Cup 15
Goals: League 90, FA Cup 13
Debut: 15 November 1947 v Northampton Town (a) won 2–1
Manager: 1957–58

Also played for: Burnley, Everton, Arsenal, Chelsea, Brentford, England (23 caps)
Also managed: Brentford, Kettering Town

Make no mistake, Tommy Lawton was one of the superstars of his generation. A fabulously gifted centre-forward he had the world, literally, at his feet when he chose to join Notts County in November 1947.

Business interests were a contributory factor, as was Tommy's love of a challenge, but it was still an astonishing coup for the Magpies to sign the striker currently in possession of the England number nine jersey. Notts were, after all, an unfashionable Third Division club making the capture even more remarkable. The transfer fee involved amounted to £20,000 – a British record. Notts paid Chelsea £15,000 for Lawton and handed over wing-half Bill Dickson in part-exchange, a player valued at £5,000.

In the twinkling of an eye Notts had shed their dowdy image and the city was encapsulated by football fever. A goalscoring debut at Northampton helped secure the side's first away win of the season. That was the first of 90 League goals Tommy scored for the 'Pies, recorded from just 151 appearances. Detractors will claim that an international forward should make an impression at that level. They are right, of course, but only if the player continues to work hard and honestly, giving nothing less than 100 percent at all times.

Tommy was the total professional and the fans loved him. Meadow Lane came alive with attendances exceeding all expectations. Over 45,000 fans saw the 5–1 home win over Swansea on Boxing Day 1947 – with their hero scoring twice. The fans were in dreamland because Notts also possessed Jackie Sewell, one of the country's other prolific marksmen. In that first season together they totalled 48 goals, yet the club could only finish sixth.

Inside the space of two years Tommy recorded six hat-tricks for the Magpies – little wonder it became known as 'the Lawton era'. On three of those occasions the number nine actually hit four goals, including four in the club record 11–1 win over Newport County in January 1949.

Fans will be united in their choice of Tommy's most memorable Notts goal – across the Trent at the City Ground, a bullet of a header that helped secure a 2–1 League victory over Nottingham Forest in December 1949. Frank Broome's deep corner was powered home with Lawton later explaining, 'I never hit a ball as hard before. Everything went exactly right. I just got clear and my jump was carrying me forward as I met the ball full on my forehead.'

Another headed goal against Forest, this time in April 1950, helped Tommy to realise one of the driving reasons behind his move to Notts – promotion, after securing the Division Three South championship.

Born in Farnworth, near Bolton, Tommy made his League debut for Burnley, aged just 16. His prodigious talents were already attracting attention and Everton signed him for £6,500 while he was still only 17. Playing alongside the legendary Dixie Dean, the young Lawton received the perfect grounding. He made his international debut in 1938 and scored a total of 22 goals in just 23 matches for England. His time at Goodison Park was halted by the outbreak of World War Two and he joined Chelsea afterwards.

Although his fine career was cruelly interrupted, Tommy still made 390 League appearances between 1936 and 1956, scoring a phenomenal 231 times. Towards the end of his playing days Tommy served as player-manager at both Brentford and Kettering Town before returning to Meadow Lane to become the Notts boss.

He later became a licensee, running the Magna Carta at Lowdham, Notts. Tommy Lawton died in 1996 and at the request of his son, Tommy junior, his ashes are on display at the National Football Museum in Preston.

Andy Legg

Date of birth: 28 July 1966, Neath

Notts County record:
Appearances: League 89, FA Cup 8, League Cup 11, Others 15
Goals: League 9, FA Cup 0, League Cup 0, Others 6
Debut: 14 August 1993 v Middlesbrough (h) lost 2–3

Also played for: Briton Ferry Athletic, Swansea City, Birmingham City, Ipswich Town, Reading, Cardiff City, Peterborough United, Wales (6 caps)

Apart from his cheery nature and will-to-win attitude Andy Legg will be remembered as the footballer who could throw the ball for miles. There was more – much more – to the Welshman's game of course, but in the history of the sport no one has been able to propel a throw-in as far as he could.

'When I was about 12 or 13, I realised I could throw the ball much further than anyone of my age', he reveals. 'I played a lot of tennis at the time and don't know if that helped at all, but it was something that certainly served me well over the years. No one ever really taught me how to throw the ball so far, although Terry Yorath made me practice with a "medicine ball" during my time at Swansea.'

Andy's ability to hurl the ball into a crowded penalty area proved to be a valuable asset for many sides and contributed to a famous goal in Notts County's history. It also earned him a place in the record books.

'One day at the Vetch Field I did a piece for *Shoot* magazine and they measured that I'd thrown the ball 49 metres. Then I was invited to try for a place in the *Guinness Book of Records* by doing it under test conditions at Wembley Stadium. I was only allowed a four-step run-up and threw 43 metres the first time. That set the record and I broke it, before an England match against Brazil, when I threw 44.6 metres.'

Andy joined Notts from Swansea, in the summer of 1993, for a fee of £275,000. 'Eight clubs had expressed an interest in signing me and, although Notts were offering me the least money, I was impressed by the friendliness of the place and knew it would be the right choice for me.'

Although the club narrowly missed out on a place in the play-offs, Andy's first season at Meadow Lane did produce a couple of highlights. 'I will always remember the 2–1 win over Forest. Although we came out on top I just thought it was a fantastic day for the city. Both sets of fans mingled and the atmosphere was brilliant. I'd only been used to the Swansea versus Cardiff derbies, which were often spoilt by the intense hatred they had for each other.'

The Anglo-Italian Cup competition also gave Andy the chance to play at Wembley for the first time. Although the side went down to Brescia, they were able to return the following season and lift the trophy. County's winning goal that day is still shrouded in mystery, but was initiated by a well-aimed set-piece. 'I threw the ball into the Ascoli area and thought it had gone straight into the net. Tony Agana claimed he'd got a touch and fortunately the referee felt so and allowed the goal. I still feel it went straight in though.'

Winning at Wembley was undoubtedly the highlight of Andy's time at Notts, although the next stage of his career was being monitored during his time at Meadow Lane. 'Colin Murphy kept telling me I was good enough to play for my country and he persuaded Bobby Gould, Wales' international manager, to come and watch me. Shortly afterwards I was awarded my first Welsh cap, but by then I'd completed my move to Birmingham.'

Andy went on to enjoy a long and successful career, clocking up over 700 first-team appearances. Usually playing at either left-back or on the left side of midfield, he enjoyed the 'versatile' tag he was given, and revelled in a number of other positions later in his career. He spent the 2004–05 season as player-coach at Peterborough United and was still a regular first-team player, despite passing his 38th birthday. In April 2005 he revealed that he was retiring from the game, as he had been diagnosed with a rare form of throat cancer. A successful operation to remove a tumour on his neck heralded the start of a lengthy period of radiotherapy. Despite his own health concerns, Andy saw the benefit in the publicity his illness had generated. 'If reading about my case raised awareness in people then I'm delighted. It's so important to seek medical advice and get treatment early.'

With his football career temporarily on hold Andy revealed he will never regret his decision to join the Magpies. 'It's where I met my wife Lucy. We live in Lambley, so hopefully I'll be able to follow their fortunes a little more closely now.'

Mick Leonard

Date of birth: 9 May 1959, Carshalton, Surrey

Notts County record:

Appearances: League 204, FA Cup 20, League Cup 15, Others 15

Debut: 15 September 1979 v Luton Town (h) drew 0–0

Also played for: Epsom & Ewell, Halifax Town, Chesterfield, Instant Dict (Hong Kong), South China FC (China)

There are many that believe that goalkeepers are not very smart but Mick Leonard is on a mission to prove them wrong. The former County goalie has spent more than a decade working outside the UK and has more qualifications than your average university 'don'.

Since packing his own gloves away, Mick has been actively involved in the development of many other young hopefuls, reminiscent of the days when he began his own League career with Halifax Town.

His first-team debut came at just 17 years of age and he had already played in 69 League matches before a crisis brought him to Meadow Lane. County's number one, Raddy Avramovic, sustained an injury and his deputy, Colin King, was already sidelined with a broken leg, so Jimmy Sirrel stepped into the transfer market to recruit the promising Leonard for a fee of £30,000.

A clean sheet in each of his first two matches, against Luton Town and Swansea City, was a fine way for any goalie to begin at his new club and Mick caught the eye with his coolness under pressure as well as his fine shot-stopping.

Once the Yugoslav regained full fitness it was a case of watching and waiting for Mick – as well as learning from the vastly-experienced Raddy. First-team appearances were restricted – just four in the promotion season of 1980–81 and just one a year later (a 0–6 thrashing against Aston Villa in the FA Cup).

Mick's time did arrive though and he was an important part of the squad for almost a decade. His best run in the side came between August 1987 and February 1989 when he put together a run of 71 consecutive League games. This was only broken when the club accepted a bid from Chesterfield for his services. During his five years with the Saltergate club he played in the 1990 play-off final at Wembley, as well as being appointed club skipper.

Asia beckoned, though, and in 1994 Mick embarked on a seven-year adventure during which he played and coached in both Hong Kong and China. While in Hong Kong he represented the Hong Kong League XI in 'internationals' against Sweden, Poland, Switzerland and Yugoslavia.

While he was still primarily regarded as a player during this period, Mick was also working hard at obtaining the necessary coaching and educational qualifications he would need for the day when he stopped playing. His dedication paid off handsomely as he emerged with his UEFA 'A' Licence, English FA Advanced Coaching Licence, a FIFA Goalkeeping Certificate, an FA Diploma in the Treatment and Management of Sports Injuries and a postgraduate diploma in sports and recreational management.

After spending some time back in England working as the academy goalkeeping coach across the River Trent, Mick was lured to New Zealand in 2003 to take up the post of national goalkeeping coach. Like Avramovic, his long-time mentor, Mick has become an outstanding coach on the international scene.

His role ensures he is actively involved in all aspects of goalkeeping work at the National Regional Academies, for both males and females. In addition, for the 2005–06 New Zealand season, Mick has joined the coaching staff at the prominent Auckland club side, NZ Knights.

Leon Leuty

Date of birth: 23 October 1920, Meole Brace, Shropshire

Died: 15 December 1955

Notts County record:

Appearances: League 188, FA Cup 12

Goals: League 3, FA Cup 1

Debut: 23 September 1950 v Preston North End (h) lost 1–3

Also played for: Derby County, Bradford Park Avenue

Notts' rich and colourful history is illuminated by a number of outstanding, commanding central defenders. Leon Leuty would stand comparison with any of them.

Leon was a month short of his 30th birthday when he signed for Notts County, having won an FA Cup winners' medal, captained the England 'B' side and represented the Football League side earlier in his career. He had also played in an 'unofficial international' during the war and was considered unlucky not to receive a full England cap.

Standing only 5ft 10in in height, Leon was surprisingly dominant in the air but his real strength was in the style and composure he displayed. He was a delightful player to watch but a real handful to play against. Opposition centre-forwards rarely met anyone so resolute in the tackle. The supporters loved him!

The war years disrupted a footballing career which was developing well. He had signed for Derby County as an amateur and found work at Rolls-Royce. Leon made his first few appearances for Notts 'guesting' in wartime friendlies but he re-signed for Derby and played at centre-half in their cup-winning side of 1946. After more than 150 League and cup games for the Rams, Leon signed for Bradford Park Avenue in March 1950. The fee was £20,000, which the Yorkshire side quickly recouped, selling their asset to Notts six months later for a profit of £5,000.

Leuty's presence in the side lifted all around him. Club skipper Tommy Lawton resigned the captaincy in favour of the defender. Leon also took over penalty-taking duties briefly, netting two of his four Notts goals from the spot.

Throughout the majority of his time with the Magpies, the club languished in the lower half of Division Two. But for Leuty's leadership, organisational ability and tactical awareness the club may well have spiralled down into the lower leagues. As it was, there were considerable signs of improvement as a seventh-place finish was achieved at the end of the 1954–55 season. Hopes of a promotion push were definitely on the Meadow Lane agenda. As it was, the season will be remembered only for tragedy.

After just two matches of the 1955–56 season, Leon complained of a shoulder injury. Rest failed to bring about any improvement in the condition so the defender went to hospital for checks. His condition deteriorated rapidly. Although he was able to watch a couple of games during November, the club skipper was taken seriously ill and diagnosed with leukaemia.

Leon Leuty was aged just 35 when he passed away on 15 December 1955. He had played in exactly 200 League and cup games for Notts.

Jimmy Logan

Date of birth: 24 June 1870, Troon, Scotland
Died: 25 May 1896

Notts County record:
Appearances: League 41, FA Cup 7, Others 8
Goals: League 31, FA Cup 6, Others 0
Debut: 5 October 1893 v Grimsby Town (h) won 3–0

Also played for: Aston Villa, Dundee, Newcastle United, Loughborough Town

FA Cup final hat-tricks have been a surprisingly rare commodity over the years. Since the competition began in 1872 only three players have managed to achieve the feat. Most fans will have read, or seen television pictures, heralding the achievements of Blackpool's Stan Mortenson in the perhaps inappropriately titled 'Matthews Final' of 1953. The other two players are not so well known. Even the most devoted football afficionado might struggle to come up with the name of Billy Townley of Blackburn Rovers, who in 1890 became the first player to achieve the feat against Sheffield Wednesday.

Notts County supporters, quite rightly, take immense pride in the achievement of Jimmy Logan, who is the third member of this rather exclusive set. The Scot joined Notts from Aston Villa for £15 in the autumn of 1893 and scored twice on his debut against Grimsby Town. He followed that up with goals in each of his next two matches and a hat-trick against Port Vale to make it seven goals in four games – not a bad signing!

In League games Jimmy averaged a goal a game for his first season – 21 from 21, including another treble, this time against Northwich Victoria. Although he was not particularly tall, standing at just 5ft 8Qw in, the Scot possessed great pace and had an uncanny ability to find the back of the net.

Notts finished third in Division Two but the disappointment of missing out on promotion was tempered by another great run in the FA Cup. Penalty kicks had become a recent introduction into the game and Jimmy is credited with converting the first Notts goal from the spot during a second round tie, played away at Burton Wanderers, on 10 February 1894. Further wins over Nottingham Forest and Blackburn Rovers saw County reach the final for the second time in four seasons. The opponents this time were Bolton Wanderers, a First Division side and overwhelming favourites to clinch the tie.

The match was played at Everton's Goodison Park ground and Notts prepared for it by spending several days relaxing at West Kirby in Cheshire. Sandy Ferguson, who had played for County in the 1891 final, died just before the match. Whether this motivated the players or not is unclear, but they made all the running and went ahead through a goal from Arthur Watson after 19 minutes. Bolton's hopes of staging a fight-back were soon extinguished as Jimmy scored his first in the 31st minute. Two up at the break, Notts already had one hand on the silverware and they cemented victory with further goals from their ace striker. With a wonderful piece of individualism Logan made it 3–0 after 67 minutes and three minutes later he reached his hat-trick with a spectacular volley.

Although the Lancashire side scored a late consolation, the FA Cup was on its way to Nottingham – as County celebrated becoming the first side from outside the top division to achieve the feat. The town went wild as the train carrying the returning heroes arrived home. Fans lined the streets and a brass band played – rarely had such a scene been witnessed.

Jimmy Logan was never to experience such a high again. He was unable to fully recapture his goalscoring form the following season, although he did score 10 goals, including his fourth hat-trick for the club, this time against Walsall. The Scot returned home to play for Dundee but then moved south again, playing briefly for Newcastle United before joining up with Loughborough Town. Travelling to play Newton Heath in Manchester, the Loughborough side somehow mislaid their kit. Unable to acquire any other, they played the match in their everyday clothes, which were then worn for the return train journey. Jimmy Logan caught a chill, which turned to pneumonia and, just short of his 26th birthday, he passed away.

Notts County's FA Cup final hat-trick hero was buried in a pauper's grave in Loughborough.

Bert Loxley

Date of birth: 3 February 1934, Bonsall, Derbyshire

Notts County record:

Appearances: League 245, FA Cup 13, League Cup 8
Goals: League 9, FA Cup 1, League Cup 1
Debut: 30 April 1955 v Ipswich Town (h) won 2–1

Also played for: Bonsall FC, Mansfield Town, Lincoln City
Managed: Lincoln City

There are not too many footballers who could play in three separate relegation campaigns and still be held in the highest of esteem by the supporters of that club. Bert Loxley gave his all for Notts County and later in life served Lincoln City with equal distinction in an off-the-field capacity.

At an early age Bert's talent shone through. In just six matches for his school first team he smashed in a prodigious 37 goals – surely a record of some sort.

With Bonsall FC, his local village side, Bert began to attract the headlines for some outstanding displays in the Rowsley and District League. A first taste of representative football came with selection for Derbyshire against Lancashire in an inter-county match. Plenty of scouts turned up to watch and he was taken for trials at a number of clubs including Coventry City, Derby County and York City. It was Notts County that held most appeal for the youngster and he turned professional after a stunning display for the club's reserve team in a match against Mansfield Town.

National Service was spent in the Army but Bert was handed his first-team debut in the final match of the 1954–55 season. He said later, 'It's a match I will always remember because it was the only time I was able to play alongside the great Leon Leuty.' Bert had to bide his time before establishing himself in the Notts team but he made 13 appearances the following season, netting his first goal in a home win over Bury.

Tall and fair-haired, Bert's first few years as a professional were spent in the 'old-fashioned' wing-half position but later he switched to centre-back, with similar effect. Strong in the tackle and forceful in the air, his consistency was to be admired for over a decade.

Successive relegations between 1957 and 1959 saw Notts drop from the old Second Division into the bottom flight. Not for the first time, nor the last, things were looking grim at Meadow Lane. The supporters needed a lift and it came instantly. Bert made 36 appearances as the Magpies bounced back at the first time of asking, finishing second in Division Four.

Bert participated in County's first ever match in the Football League Cup in 1960. He did not score often but his only FA Cup goal for the club saved huge embarrassment. A looping header thwarted non-League Margate's hopes of an upset and secured a replay back at Meadow Lane, which Notts won.

In 1962, Bert was a member of the squad that enjoyed the club's centenary celebrations – there was another season of disappointment just around the corner though. In 1963–64, Notts finished bottom of the Third Division and, after clocking up almost 250 League appearances for County, Bert moved on to join up with Mansfield Town.

After a sole season at Field Mill he left to take up the role of trainer/coach at Lincoln City. On nine occasions he was called out of retirement to play for the Imps before finally hanging up his boots for good. Bert became Lincoln's version of a 'Jack Wheeler', filling the posts of trainer, coach and physiotherapist, as well as taking over as first-team manager during the 1970–71 season. He was rewarded with a testimonial match 10 years later when Nottingham Forest sent their European Cup-winning side to Sincil Bank to honour him.

Loved in Lincoln as much as he is in Nottingham, Bert Loxley was one of football's genuinely nice guys.

Gary Lund

Date of birth: 13 September 1964, Grimsby

Notts County record:
Appearances: League 248, FA Cup 16, League Cup 18, Others 34
Goals: League 62, FA Cup 4, League Cup 5, Others 8
Debut: 15 August 1987 v Wigan Athletic (h) drew 4–4

Also played for: Grimsby Town, Hull City, Lincoln City, Chesterfield

Gary Lund has one major regret about his days with Notts County. 'I spent eight and a half very happy years with the club and would have loved to have stayed there for a decade. Not for a testimonial, or anything like that – I'd have just liked to have done 10 years.'

The forward almost arrived at Meadow Lane by accident. 'I'd been at Lincoln when they were relegated from the Football League. It was the first season of that happening and there was a clause in everyone's contract that they could go on the transfer list. I'd got one or two other options but when I talked to Notts I felt they were a club with lots of potential. Derek Pavis and John Barnwell had just arrived and they'd made one or two decent signings.'

In his first season with Notts, Gary scored 20 goals. 'It just seemed whenever I played I managed to score but I didn't really consider myself as a regular at any stage.' Despite his own doubts, Gary was becoming a firm favourite with the fans, especially after hitting a hat-trick against Rotherham United. 'I can't remember any of the goals', he admits. 'I know I've still got the ball in the loft but it's flat now and all the signatures have faded.'

The arrival of Neil Warnock gave the club – and Gary – a chance to go to Wembley but the initial feeling was not one of joy. 'To be honest we were feeling cheated because we didn't want to be in the play-offs. We finished third behind the two Bristol clubs but were miles ahead of anyone else and felt we should have gone up automatically.'

Nevertheless, the day itself was memorable. 'It's every player's boyhood dream to play at Wembley and I was no different. Possibly they devalued the stadium a little by holding so many matches there but when we went it was still a novelty and it was fantastic to cap it all by winning.'

A year later Gary looked on from the sidelines, not included in the side for the win over Brighton. 'Dave Regis had come in and was being given a run in the side but obviously I was as pleased as anyone that we won.' Earlier that season Gary scored the goal for which he is still best remembered by County fans – the FA Cup winner against Manchester City. 'The more the week went on, the more we fancied our chances. The snowy conditions seemed conducive for a spot of giant-killing.'

As the players 'warmed up' by sledging and snowballing in Wollaton Park, there was a serious doubt about the game going ahead. 'I remember there being an appeal for supporters to go to the ground and help clear away the snow. The chairman was promising free tickets to everyone who helped and not surprisingly he ended up with a full house.' With around 10 minutes to go, and the match scoreless, Gary got his chance. 'The ball just ricocheted to me from about six yards out and I hit it left-footed past the man on the line. The place just erupted!'

Gary's most consistent season was 1993–94 when he played in 61 of the club's 62 games, scoring a total of 18 times. Five of those goals came in the Anglo-Italian Cup. 'Everyone knew that it didn't carry the same importance as some other competitions but it was still rewarding to get through to Wembley again, even if we didn't play as well as I thought we could have.'

After leaving Notts, Gary spent a brief period with Chesterfield, though a back injury ruined any hope of a regular run in the side. With partner Chris Royston he had also opened an estate agents and decided to quit football to fully concentrate on his business activities.

Royston and Lund have offices in West Bridgford and Bingham, which is near enough for Gary to keep a close eye on the Magpies' fortunes. 'The club have had some dodgy times recently and it's quite distressing for ex-players to see them suffering. I just hope they can turn things around quickly because I really believe they should at least be playing in the Championship.'

Arthur Mann

Date of birth: 23 January 1948, Burntisland, Fife
Died: 3 February 1999

Notts County record:

Appearances: League 253, FA Cup 14, League Cup 16, Others 9
Goals: League 21, FA Cup 1, League Cup 2, Others 1
Debut: 12 August 1972 v Shrewsbury Town (a) drew 0–0

Also played for: Hearts, Manchester City, Blackpool, Shrewsbury Town, Mansfield Town, Boston United, Telford United, Kettering Town
Managed: Boston United

Arthur Mann was a real players' player – a tireless workhorse who always put the club's needs before his own. During a seven-year spell at Meadow Lane, he notched up more than 250 League appearances and helped the club into Division Two by winning promotion in his first season.

Known as 'Archie' to his mates, he had a proven pedigree by the time he joined Notts. He had graduated through the ranks at Hearts and appeared in their side that lost in the 1968 Scottish Cup final to Dunfermline. A move to Manchester City followed in November of the same year. While with City, Arthur picked up a League Cup winners' medal, helping to defeat West Bromwich Albion 2–1, after extra time, at Wembley Stadium.

The battle for first-team places at Maine Road was intense and Arthur was restricted to just 35 League appearances, spread over almost four years. Needing to play regular first-team football, the Scot went out on loan to Blackpool, before accepting an offer to join the Magpies in time for the start of the 1972–73 season. Although much of Arthur's career had been spent at left-back, he was just as comfortable further forward and slotted into the Notts midfield with comparative ease.

In his first season with the club Archie played in 42 League matches, scoring just once, although he did score in the FA Cup as the 'black and white stripes' progressed to round five, before going down to Chelsea at Stamford Bridge. Throughout the mid-1970s, Arthur was a model of consistency and regularly selected for the Magpies. His limitless energy levels, and the ability to run all day, earned him the respect and admiration from fans and colleagues alike.

Jeff Grain, from Breaston in Derbyshire, has followed Notts for over 40 years and believes Arthur was one of the club's all-time greats. 'He really could play anywhere', says Jeff. 'A true utility player, who turned in outstanding performances in many different positions. Arthur was outstanding in the 1976–77 season and deservedly won the Player of the Year award.'

Arthur eventually left Meadow Lane in 1979, signing for Shrewsbury. The move was not totally to his liking and within four months he was back in Nottinghamshire, playing for Mansfield Town. After completing over a century of appearances for the Stags, Arthur's determination to continue playing saw him move into the non-League game, with spells at Boston United, Telford United and Kettering Town.

During a second spell at Boston he took over as manager and led the side to the FA Trophy final at Wembley. He then linked up with Alan Buckley to form a successful managerial partnership – Arthur becoming Buckley's assistant at Grimsby Town and later at West Bromwich Albion.

Tragedy struck in February 1999, when Arthur Mann was fatally injured in an accident with a fork-lift truck. He was just 51.

Don Masson

Date of birth: 26 August 1946, Banchory, near Aberdeen

Notts County record:
Appearances: League 401, FA Cup 16, League Cup 23, Others 13
Goals: League 92, FA Cup 3, League Cup 1, Others 1
Debut: 14 September 1968 v Darlington (a) lost 2–3

Also played for: Middlesbrough, Queens Park Rangers, Derby County, Minnesota Kicks (USA), Scotland (17 caps)

Don Masson would have very few rivals in any poll to nominate Notts County's greatest ever midfielder. To most fans he was 'The Don' – to the rest, he was 'Masson the Magnificent'. Like all the truly gifted performers, he seemed to have so much more time than anyone around him.

The young Don grew up in a small village called Banchory, 18 miles from Aberdeen. 'The Queen would often pass through on the train on her way to Balmoral. All of us school kids would be taken down to the station to wave Union Jacks at her. It didn't go down too well, as we wanted to wave the Scottish flag!'

After helping Middlesbrough achieve promotion in 1967, Don suddenly found himself down the pecking order. 'Three into two wouldn't go and Johnny Crossan and Eric McMordie were being preferred as the central midfielders. I just wanted to play football – I didn't really know much about Notts County but they promised me first-team football, so I signed along with Bob Worthington – they got the pair of us for £7,000.'

Billy Gray was the Notts' manager but within a couple of weeks he had gone and Jack Wheeler was put in temporary charge. 'Jack made me captain when we were 90th out of 92 clubs', says Don.

The Masson magic began – he had scored on his Notts debut and very quickly established the utmost respect from teammates and supporters alike, even if he was not the most popular member of the dressing room. 'It's true I wasn't always the most jovial person around. I'd like to think I'm different now but I was always pretty intense as a footballer. I cared about the game and wouldn't tolerate those who didn't give the same level of commitment. I wanted to be the best and if that meant going in early to do weight training or extra sprints, then I'd be there.'

Jimmy Sirrel's arrival at County signalled the start of the so-called 'Golden Era', with Don as his shining light and inspiration. 'The Division Four title was a particularly enjoyable season. Tony Hateley came back to the club and we had gates of over 20,000 at Meadow Lane.' Don was around to skipper the side to their next promotion before leaving to experience top-flight football with QPR and Derby County, as well as going on to captain his homeland.

His 17th and final cap came during the 1978 World Cup Finals in Argentina and will be remembered for an important spot-kick miss against Peru. 'I've lost count of the number of Scottish fans I've apologised to for that', he confesses. 'I sometimes have to remind them that I did score an important one in a World Cup qualifier against Wales!'

Back for a second spell with Notts, Don completed the full set of promotions, as he led the side into Division One, although he missed out on the significant moment. 'I missed the match at Chelsea through injury and was so upset I couldn't bear to go and watch. To take my mind off things I drove up to Middlesbrough to see my sister but was told the good news at full-time. I drove back south and was back at Meadow Lane to greet the players as they returned – it was some night, what I can remember of it!' Don's appearance and goal tally for Notts stands comparison with all but a select few. Despite notching so many vital goals himself, it is another strike that gives him most pleasure. 'A goal scored by Gordon Mair at Ipswich was almost the perfect team goal. Virtually everybody had a touch – a brilliant goal.'

The man who wanted to be the best came 'very, very close' to achieving it but had one footballing ambition left unfulfilled. 'I always fancied managing Notts County. It would only have been them – no other club – but for one reason or another I didn't push myself for it. It would have been the icing on the cake for me.'

After many years running The Gallery Hotel in Nottingham, Don can now be found at The Grange at Elton, on the A52, where there's an especially warm welcome waiting for any County fan. 'I really do love it when football fans come and stay with us. As a player you don't always take in what your achievements have meant to so many other people. It's touching when supporters want to talk about things that happened 30 years ago.'

Whether it is 30 years or 300 years, County fans will never forget Don Masson.

Iain McCulloch

Date of birth: 28 December 1954, Kilmarnock

Notts County record:

Appearances: League 215, FA Cup 11, League Cup 16, Others 17

Goals: League 51, FA Cup 2, League Cup 1, Others 0

Debut: 15 August 1978 v Scunthorpe United (h) won 3–0 (League Cup)

Also played for: Hurlford Juniors, Kilmarnock, Plessey

Iain McCulloch was Notts County's 'Braveheart' during a glorious era in the club's history. The charismatic Scot was idolised by the fans who worshipped his full-blooded commitment every time he pulled on the black and white jersey.

Having agreed to move to the 'Lane', Iain's transfer was unexpectedly put on hold after his Kilmarnock side went on a decent run in the Scottish Cup. 'We beat Celtic and then drew Rangers in the quarter-finals so I stayed at Killie a little longer than planned', he explains. The move went through eventually and Notts looked after their new 'import' by housing Iain and his wife in the Albany Hotel. 'It was all a bit overwhelming – I didn't even know which knife to use!' says the wisecracking Scot. 'Everybody was so welcoming, so friendly. It was all very homely. The only thing that unnerved me was trying to understand Jimmy Sirrel's accent – and he was Scottish like me!'

Iain began his days at Notts by playing wide on the right before being switched up front. His partnership with Trevor Christie was instrumental in the side achieving promotion at the end of the 1979–80 season. 'Both Trevor and myself were prepared to work hard. We got on well together, on and off the pitch. Basically, I think it was down to us having respect for each other.'

Iain scored Notts' last goal in Division Two at the end of the promotion year and then had the satisfaction of opening his account with the winner at Aston Villa, as the side celebrated their return to the top flight.

The Scot managed one hat-trick for the 'Pies – away at West Brom in a game he should not have played in. 'I had flu and rang in to say I wasn't fit. The gaffer (Jimmy Sirrel) told me I'd run it off but I told him not to be silly. It was agreed that I'd travel and we'd see how I felt when we arrived. I had a bad throat and was running a temperature but despite my protests Jimmy put me on the team sheet.' Iain recalls how ill he felt. 'I felt awful for the first 20 minutes but then began to run it off. In the second half it all went right, a header in the six-yard box, a pass from Gordon Mair which I put in the top-left corner and then a pass from Benjy which went in the top right. Perfect – although I threw up on the bus on the way home!'

He recalls his best Notts goal with great fondness. 'It was away against Spurs and I beat Ray Clemence from about 40 yards.' They were great times for the club and local derbies were greeted with great anticipation. Unfortunately for Iain, the 3–2 home win over Forest in December 1982 was marred by a card-happy official. 'Everyone was really hyped up for the game but I was sent off for a challenge that looked worse than it was. I cut inside Bryn Gunn, he nicked the ball and I just caught him. It certainly wasn't deliberate but the referee thought otherwise!'

Iain had scored County's first goal that day on the way to becoming top scorer for the second season running, but tragedy struck in April 1984. Playing at home against Manchester United, Iain was involved in a collision with Gary Bailey, the visitor's goalkeeper, which left him with a badly broken leg. 'I didn't feel too bad in the dressing room or in the treatment room but it was pretty painful by the time I'd got to hospital. After six months they had to put a pin in it, then they had to do a bone graft.'

After his enforced retirement Iain remained in Nottingham, where he has run his own double-glazing business for many years. He has played and coached in local non-League circles for many years, first with Plessey and latterly with Arnold Town.

Still immensely popular whenever he returns to Meadow Lane, Iain has a refreshing outlook on life. 'When I wake up in the morning, open the curtains and see the sun shining, you've got to be happy!'

Eric McManus

Date of birth: 14 November 1950, Limavady

Notts County record:

Appearances: League 229, FA Cup 9, League Cup 13, Others 14

Debut: 7 November 1972 v Bristol Rovers (a) lost 0–1

Also played for: Coventry City, Stoke City, Bradford City, Tranmere Rovers

Managed: Bromsgrove Rovers

A likeable Irishman safely protected Notts County's goal for almost seven years during the 1970s.

After three seasons with Coventry City, Eric McManus had moved to Meadow Lane in search of first-team football. He had to wait for his opportunity, though, with Roy Brown firmly in possession of the green jersey. Eric's first season with the Magpies ended with the joy of promotion from the Third Division. One loan appearance in the autumn and starts in the final three matches were his only involvement but he had slotted into the County way of life and was popular with his teammates.

The following season saw a changing of the guard as far as the goalkeeping position was concerned. Out of the 42 League matches, Eric played in 34, as Notts claimed a respectable 10th place finish.

In March 1975 the Magpies brought up a historical milestone by becoming the first side to play in 3,000 League matches. Fittingly, the match was played at Meadow Lane and the opponents were Nottingham Forest. In front of over 20,000 fans 'Supermac' pulled off some outstanding saves to earn Notts a precious point.

Later the same year the club embarked upon its most successful run in the League Cup competition. Famous wins over Leeds United and Everton took them into the last eight, where they went down by the only goal at Newcastle United. Cruelly, Eric was credited with the decider, with it going down as an own goal after it slipped from his grasp.

In each of the next three seasons Eric was extremely consistent. He appeared in every League and cup game between 27 March 1976 and 5 May 1979 – an unbroken run of 162 matches – truly a phenomenal achievement. Deservedly, his form won him the Player of the Year award at the end of the 1978–79 season.

Sadly for Notts, outstanding performances attract the headlines and Stoke City's pursuit of Eric was rewarded when they signed him during the summer of 1979. His stay at the Victoria Ground was badly hampered by an elbow injury and he was soon on the move again, playing for both Bradford City and Tranmere Rovers before turning to coaching. He spent nine years working with the academy players at Walsall, before moving to Derby County in June 1998 as Director of Recruitment for their youth academy. In November 2000 he tried his hand at management, briefly taking over at Ryman League side, Bromsgrove Rovers.

For several years Eric has run his own freelance goalkeeper coaching school, enabling him to help out at Loughborough University as well as further stints at his old clubs Coventry City, Derby County and Walsall again.

Although Eric played at a time when Notts County and success were not often to be found hand in hand, he was a firm favourite with the fans and his reliability was never questioned. Since hanging up his boots he has passed on his immense knowledge of the game to thousands of youngsters – there can be no greater testimony.

Ian McParland

Date of birth: 4 October 1961, Edinburgh

Notts County record:

Appearances: League 221, FA Cup 17, League Cup 16, Others 13

Goals: League 69, FA Cup 9, League Cup 5, Others 7

Debut: 27 December 1980 v Preston North End (a) drew 2–2

Also played for: Ormiston Primrose, Hull City, Dunfermline Athletic, Northampton Town, Instant Dict (Hong Kong), Eastern Athletic (Hong Kong)

Ian McParland does not have time for any footballer who complains about hard work. He spent two years getting up at four in the morning to work down the mines at Monkton Hall Colliery. 'I'd spent six months at Sunderland as an apprentice but was home-sick', he admits. 'I come from a small mining village so digging for coal seemed the way to make a living.'

An opportunity to make a name for himself as a footballer seemed to have gone begging. 'I played with people like Allan Brown and Mick Docherty at Sunderland – Bobby Kerr was there, right at the end of his career, but I couldn't wait to get back home.' When another chance presented itself Ian was ready. 'Willie Stewart, Notts County's scout in Scotland, saw me play in a Scottish Junior Cup match and asked if I'd be interested in a trial. Although it still took me time to adjust to being away from home, I liked Nottingham as a place to live and the people were all very friendly so I was determined to make a go of it.'

Injuries and suspensions meant a surprise first-team debut, as a substitute, while still aged only 19. Over the next couple of seasons he flitted in and out of the side, learning his trade and listening to the wise words of advice from the likes of Jimmy Sirrel and Howard Wilkinson.

His first goal for the club was a while in coming – almost two and a half years and 26 appearances – after his debut. The wait, though, was worthwhile as it came against Manchester United on the final day of the 1982–83 season, helping the side to a 3–2 home win. 'In those days I played out wide on the right but it was nice to get that first goal. John Chiedozie gave it to me 25 yards out and I just hit it and hoped for the best. A lad called Jeff Wealands was in goal for United that day but he had no chance. It went right into the top corner – a last-minute winner, the fans went wild!'

Notts were relegated at the end of each of the next two seasons but their arrival in Division Three coincided with Ian moving to a more central striking role. The goals began to fly in, as he finished top scorer for the Magpies for four consecutive seasons. His purple patch included a haul of 27 goals in 1986–87 and 28 the year after. Nicknamed 'Charlie', the Scot smashed three hat-tricks for County, against Port Vale and Fulham in the League and against Mansfield Town in the League Cup.

Apart from his debut goal, Ian recalls a stunner against Sunderland. 'I hit it just right – it curled in from the edge of the box. Mind you, we won 6–1 that day – they were so bad even Pedro Richards scored!'

After leaving Meadow Lane, Ian played briefly for Hull City and Dunfermline but a niggling hip injury restricted his performances. 'I was told to pack in playing because of my hip but was given the opportunity to go and play in Hong Kong, which I did for a couple of years and thoroughly enjoyed.' Ian then decided to give way to his own stubbornness. 'My old teammate, Mick Leonard, used to study hard for all his coaching badges. I used to say, "Not me – I've played the game so why do I need qualifications?" I realised, though, that football was all I knew and that I'd better take the badges if I wanted to stay in the game.'

After spending some time coaching youngsters in America, Ian returned to Nottingham and was given a job at the City Ground by Paul Hart, looking after Forest's Under-13s. By the end of the 2004–05 season, he had spent eight seasons on the club's coaching staff and had been elevated to the position of reserve-team coach.

Gary McSwegan

Date of birth: 24 September 1970, Glasgow

Notts County record:

Appearances: League 62, FA Cup 5, League Cup 6, Others 6

Goals: League 21, FA Cup 1, League Cup 3, Others 1

Debut: 14 August 1993 v Middlesbrough (h) lost 2–3

Also played for: Rangers, Dundee United, Hearts, Barnsley, Luton Town, Kilmarnock, Ross County, Scotland (2 caps)

No Notts County fan will forget 12 February 1994. Twice European Champions and cross-Trent rivals Nottingham Forest were beaten at Meadow Lane by two goals to one. Amidst euphoric scenes 'Sir Charlie Palmer' scored his famous late winner and the old foe were vanquished. All County supporters claim to remember it vividly but there was another Magpie on the scoresheet that day and it was the name 'McSwegan' that was being sung around the city's streets that night.

Gary McSwegan played a blinder, hitting a post and then scoring the opening goal. 'I've still got the match on video and look at it from time to time', says the Scot. 'After all Forest's recent success we were very much the poor relations of the two sides but it gave us all a great lift to win that match.'

The breakthrough came after 58 minutes and Gary recalls it clearly. 'Michael Johnson played a long ball down the left. I cut inside Steve Chettle, beat Colin Cooper and fired low inside Mark Crossley's right-hand post. In all it took just three touches from receiving it to scoring.'

Gary had joined Notts the previous summer from Glasgow Rangers, having won a Scottish Cup medal by sitting the match out as an unused substitute. 'I just felt it was time to move on. I'd been at Rangers since I was 11 and was desperate for first-team football. Notts County offered that to me. I came down and met the Chairman and Mick Walker, the manager, and was delighted to sign. I saw it as a fresh challenge and have absolutely no regrets about making the move.'

A succession of hamstring injuries disrupted Gary's two years at Meadow Lane but he has plenty of happy memories of his days as a 'Pie. 'I've still got the ball I scored a hat-trick against Derby County with and it was a great experience to play at Wembley in the Anglo-Italian Cup final against Brescia. I scored a few decent goals against the likes of Middlesbrough, Newcastle and Spurs as well. I have to say I really enjoyed my time in Nottingham and the fans were very kind.'

Gary returned to Scotland to join Dundee United early in the 1995–96 season. A later move to Hearts coincided with the best form of his career and international recognition. He played twice for Scotland in October 1999 against Bosnia and Lithuania.

'As a boyhood Rangers fan and former player, it was brilliant to make my international debut at Ibrox, even though I was only on as a sub for a few minutes. But I started the next match, at Hampden, and scored in a 3-0 win. I felt that I was very much part of Craig Brown's plans and he put me on the bench for the European Championship play-off match at Wembley against England. Craig, of course, left after that and I wasn't selected again.'

Gary joined Ross County, one of the emerging forces in Scottish football, in the summer of 2004. Ten years on, another set of County fans are able to recreate those famous chants of 'McSwegan, McSwegan!'

David McVay

Date of birth: 5 March 1955, Workington

Notts County record:

Appearances: League 113, FA Cup 4, League Cup 8, Others 5
Goals: League 2, FA Cup 0, League Cup 1, Others 0
Debut: 25 August 1973 v Crystal Palace (a) won 4–1

Also played for: Peterborough United, Torquay United, Lincoln City, Boston United

The great Socrates apart, there have been few outstanding, bearded footballers – by his own admission David McVay was no exception!

As part of Jimmy Sirrel's squad during the mid-1970s, David served Notts County during one of their less glamorous periods, a time when team spirit and togetherness were more important than a sponsor's cheque or a transfer abroad.

The former Fairham Comprehensive schoolboy had taken his 'A' Levels and seemed destined for a higher seat of learning before being taken on by Notts. 'I may well have gone to university or teacher training college', David admits. 'But I was given the chance by Notts. I actually signed for the club in the headmaster's office, with both Jimmy and Jack Dunnett present. They gave me a two-year contract so the upshot of it was that I left school and became a professional footballer. The next day I jumped on the 61A bus to Meadow Lane. I was there for 8.30 in the morning – an hour and a half before anyone else, all because my grandad had told me to get there early!'

Just six weeks after leaving school he was handed a surprise debut. 'It was the opening day of the season, away at Crystal Palace, and Willie Carlin, Les Bradd and David Needham were all suspended. We won 4–1 but I didn't really emerge with a lot of praise as it was one-all when I was substituted!'

David began his career as a central defender but was coaxed into a positional change by his manager. 'Jimmy informed me that my future was in midfield. To be fair I was never going to dislodge Stubbs or Needham at the back.'

Over the next four seasons David was out of the side almost as much as he was in it but he did have his moments. 'My first New Year's Day match was away at Sunderland – I had one of those days. It was an icy pitch and I was able to make several decent runs forward. One wag wrote in the press that I was the new Duncan Edwards. Jimmy was furious when he saw it and came out with such a mouthful of expletives in my direction – I knew he didn't rate me that highly.'

Jimmy also grew tired of David's penchant for facial hair. The beard would blossom for a period and then disappear again, usually at the first sign of an impending club fine.

Most Notts fans will feel that McVay's finest hour came in a local derby when he stifled the talents of Forest's Duncan McKenzie. 'You couldn't exactly say I had a creative game but I was given the job of man-marking him and he didn't get a kick.' The League Cup competition also brought a couple of happy memories for David. 'I played well when we beat Everton 2–0 at home and the whole team enjoyed our win at Leeds, who were almost unbeatable at that time.'

Sadly for David, all three of his senior goals for Notts came away from home but he did find the net at Meadow Lane in a prestigious first-team 'friendly' against Russian opposition. 'We drew 4–4 against Dynamo Minsk and I crossed from the left and the 'keeper flapped at it and almost threw it in.'

Although David played briefly for four other clubs, he will always be synonymous with the Magpies – particularly since he stopped playing for them! As a football writer for the *Nottingham Evening Post* he followed the club's fortunes, home and away, for several years. 'Notts were even less successful with me in the press box than they'd been with me on the field!'

During the early part of his playing career David carefully chronicled a diary of life at Meadow Lane, which he later used to good effect to write the highly-acclaimed *Steak...Diana Ross. Diary of a Football Nobody*, the inside story of life as a 'Magpie'. Along with Andy Smith, he also co-wrote *The Complete Centre Forward: The Story of Tommy Lawton*.

David McVay now works for *The Times* newspaper and is firmly established as one of this country's leading sports writers.

Steve Mildenhall

Date of birth: 13 May 1978, Swindon, Wiltshire

Notts County record:

Appearances: League 76, FA Cup 6, League Cup 5, Others 3

Goals: League Cup 1

Debut: 11 August 2001 v Port Vale (a) lost 2–4

Also played for: Swindon Town, Gloucester City, Salisbury City, Oldham Athletic, Grimsby Town

It is always nice to get your first goal for a new club and if it comes as early as your third match, then no one will have any complaints.

Fortunately, that is what happened to Steve Mildenhall. Unusually though, he was Notts County's goalkeeper when this little piece of history occurred. Had the event not actually taken place in front of 4,553 fans, then it might have been deemed the work of a fiction writer, as the story had an added twist – it was at Field Mill against local rivals Mansfield Town.

Steve had played just twice for the 'Pies after moving from home-town club Swindon Town for a fee of around £75,000. The draw for the first round of the League Cup had sent Notts to visit their county neighbours. On the night of 21 August 2001, a feast of drama and top-class entertainment was enjoyed as Danny Allsopp blasted an 11-minute hat-trick for County as the visitors came from a goal behind to lead 3–1. Things then became even worse for the Stags.

In the 34th minute Notts were awarded a free-kick midway inside their own half, a few yards to the right of centre. Motioning players upfield Steve left his area to take the kick. After carefully spotting the ball up, the 'keeper made a perfect right-footed connection and saw it sail towards the opposing end of the field, the North Stand of the Field Mill ground. Mansfield's goalkeeper, Kevin Pilkington (who himself joined Notts County in the summer of 2005), advanced towards the edge of his own area to claim the ball. Too long for forwards and defenders alike the lofted delivery looked to be an easy claim for the 'keeper but Pilkington misread the flight and allowed it to advance over his head and bounce once before dropping into the back of the net.

An error of judgement, admittedly, but Steve's moment of good fortune turned out to be hugely important as Mansfield reduced the deficit to 4–3 but County held on to advance into the next round, where further progress was halted at the hands of Manchester City.

The League Cup competition also presented Steve with another opportunity to grab a share of the limelight. In October 2003, like the rest of his colleagues, he shone in a thrilling match at Stamford Bridge, with the Premiership high-flyers eventually coming out on top, but not before Notts had threatened to produce a stunning upset.

At a towering height of 6ft 5in, Steve presented an imposing figure in the County goal. A good shot-stopper and excellent collector of crosses, he remained first choice at Meadow Lane for a couple of seasons until the club's financial situation necessitated that many players be removed from the wage bill.

Steve was allowed to leave Meadow Lane on a free transfer and he joined Oldham Athletic in December 2004. His first-team appearances were restricted at the Boundary Park club and he was allowed to join Grimsby Town for the start of the 2005–06 season.

Gary Mills

Date of birth: 11 November 1961, Northampton

Notts County record:

Appearances: League 122, FA Cup 9, League Cup 11, Others 17

Goals: League 8, FA Cup 0, League Cup 1, Others 1

Debut: 15 August 1987 v Wigan Athletic (h) drew 4–4

Manager: January 2004–November 2004

Also played for: Nottingham Forest, Derby County, Leicester City, Grantham Town, Gresley Rovers, Boston United

Also managed: Grantham Town, Kings Lynn, Tamworth, Alfreton Town

Gary Mills' career in professional football has taken him right around the East Midlands and has incorporated three spells at Meadow Lane. As a player he totted up over 150 matches in the black and white stripes before returning to the club for an all-too-brief stint as manager.

Gary joined the Magpies after becoming part of the success story on the opposite bank of the Trent. Having broken into the Nottingham Forest first team at just 17 years of age, in 1980 he became the youngest-ever player to collect a European Cup winners' medal. After an 18-match loan spell with Derby County he left the City Ground staff to join the Magpies in the summer of 1987 and celebrated his debut in a 4–4 draw against Wigan Athletic.

'I thoroughly enjoyed that first season', says Gary. 'John Barnwell was the manager and he'd put together a virtually new team. Apart from myself, players like Garry Birtles and Geoff Pike were brought in and I remember there being a really good team spirit amongst the lads.' Notts ended the season with a fourth-placed finish and a spot in the Division Three play-offs, where they were beaten by Walsall. 'It was bitterly disappointing to miss out right at the death.'

Starring on the right-hand side of midfield, Gary had been an ever-present and he made another 29 League starts during the next season before moving to Leicester City. Arguably some of his best football came during his stay with the Foxes, where he clocked up exactly 200 League appearances before re-signing for Notts in September 1994, joining in time for the second part of the Anglo-Italian adventure.

'The club had lost in the final the year before and were keen to go back. For a lot of the lads to travel abroad and play against some different opposition really was a great experience and as much as some people laughed at the competition, no one should really belittle our achievements. We went to Wembley and won a cup final – that should really say it all.'

By this stage of his career 'Millsy' was playing mainly as a full-back and looking forward to another couple of years in the game. Sadly, those hopes were dashed in December 1995 when he severed his right hamstring while playing for Notts.

The injury was serious enough to end his League career after making a total of 556 first-team appearances and scoring 44 goals, but he was able to play for a while in non-League football and take his first steps on the management ladder.

In January 2004, Gary was delighted to succeed Bill Dearden as manager of Notts County, even though the club were already deep in relegation trouble. Unable to pull themselves clear of the drop County began the 2004–05 season full of expectation but some poor results in the early stages proved critical and Gary was relieved of his position during November, having served less than 10 months in charge.

'I have to admit to feeling disgusted by the way I was treated', he admits. 'It's a big problem in the game that people aren't given long enough to do their job properly. I know I was good enough and would have turned the slide around but it's impossible to do so in such a short space of time.'

After several months working as a match summariser on local radio, Gary bounced back into club management by taking charge of Alfreton Town of the Conference North for the 2005–06 season.

Percy Mills

Date of birth: 10 January 1909, Barton-upon-Humber
Died: October 1967

Notts County record:
Appearances: League 407, FA Cup 20, Others 7
Goals: League 21, FA Cup 0, Others 0
Debut: 31 March 1928 v Barnsley (a) drew 0–0

Also played for: Barton Town

It was Adolf Hitler who finally brought the curtain down on Percy Mills' reign at Notts. For almost a dozen years the right-back berth was very firmly in the grasp of the tall Humbersider.

Percy was just 18 when he joined Notts County but he knew what to expect in making the move. His elder brother Bert, known to everyone as 'Paddy', was in his third season as the centre-forward at Meadow Lane, having formerly played for Hull City. At the time of Percy's arrival Notts were meandering just below mid-table in the Second Division. The only result of note that season had been completely unexpected – a 9–0 home mauling of Barnsley in which Paddy had helped himself to five of the goals. The brothers had little more than a year together in the same County side before Paddy went off to sign for Birmingham City. Percy was firmly established by then and, together with Charlie Bisby on the left, he helped form one of the club's most successful full-back partnerships, succeeding that of Bill Ashurst and Horace Cope.

The 1928–29 season began in spectacular fashion for the Magpies. Of the first seven matches, six were won and the other drawn. Manager Horace Henshall could certainly rely upon a settled unit as the same 11 players remained unchanged for the opening 10 matches. Disappointingly though, the side dropped too many points in the second half of the season and could only finish fifth. Hopes remained high that Notts would soon be out of the Second Division – they were, but not in the manner expected.

Relegation to Division Three was unthinkable at the outset of the 1929–30 season but the club endured one of its most miserable campaigns and finished bottom. Despite the setback, Percy Mills was considered one of the few successes.

With hindsight, the relegation enabled Notts to regroup and emerge as a stronger unit. They achieved promotion at the first time of asking, thanks chiefly to the prodigious goalscoring of Tom Keetley. The Third Division title was won by a margin of eight points from runners-up Crystal Palace. Percy played in 40 of the 42 matches but, having taken over as the club's penalty taker, he was only called upon to convert one kick, against Norwich City.

Throughout the next three seasons County were unspectacular and remained in the bottom half of the table before they again fell through the trapdoor at the end of the 1934–35 season.

During a lacklustre decade, there was little to enjoy at Meadow Lane in terms of results. Nevertheless, Percy Mills continued to perform with great consistency and had no real rivals for his place in the team.

The 1934–35 season saw Notts desert their usual black and white stripes, with a switch to home colours of chocolate and blue halves. The choice was unpopular with fans and players alike and a return to the traditional colours came quickly.

In September 1936, Notts signed the famous Scottish international Hughie Gallagher, who enabled the club to mount a concerted but ultimately unsuccessful push for another promotion.

On 8 April 1939, away at Exeter City, Percy made his 400th League appearance for the 'Pies. The club's final match of that season was his 407th. The 1939–40 season began well for Notts and they were confident of mounting a serious challenge. A home win over Bournemouth was followed by success at Cardiff City. Percy played in both matches but on 3 September 1939, the day after the win in Wales, war was declared.

Europe's unrest brought an immediate end to the Football League programme. The two matches played were officially expunged from the records, with many now showing that Percy's tally of League appearances rests at 407.

Standing at well over six feet tall, Percy possessed a venomous shot and was an accurate crosser of the ball. His main quality was as a totally committed defender, neither giving nor asking of anything other than a determined will-to-win.

Percy's grandson, the Nottingham-born Nigel Pearson, enjoyed a long and successful career in the game playing for Shrewsbury Town, Sheffield Wednesday and Middlesbrough.

David Needham

Date of birth: 21 May 1949, Leicester

Notts County record:

Appearances: League 429, FA Cup 17, League Cup 21, Others 4

Goals: League 32, FA Cup 2, League Cup 1, Others 0

Debut: 30 April 1966 v Hartlepool United (h) won 1–0

Also played for: Queens Park Rangers, Nottingham Forest, Toronto Blizzard (Canada)

Managed: Kettering Town (player-manager)

There is very little doubt that David Needham should have gone on to play for England. He really was good enough - but his incredible loyalty to Notts County meant that he remained a colossus in the lower leagues until the closing years of his career.

Most Notts supporters feel that David's partnership with Brian Stubbs was the best central defensive pairing the club have ever possessed. It is hard to disagree, given that they were teammates for eight seasons.

David was still a month away from his 17th birthday when Jack Burkitt put him into the Notts side for the final six matches of the 1965–66 season. Eleven years later he was still a regular selection as he found himself second in the table of Notts County's all-time appearance-makers, with only goalkeeper Albert Iremonger ahead of him.

While David did manage to experience a couple of promotions with Notts, for the most part the club languished in the lower echelons of the Football League. Nevertheless, he rapidly built up a reputation as being one of the best readers of the game. His ability to spot danger before it happened was immeasurable but was greatly appreciated by those around him.

Once David had claimed the number five jersey as his own, he was proud to wear it for a very long time. A terrific header of the ball, with a prodigious leap, it was somewhat surprising that he did not register his first goal for the club until December 1968, when his strike earned a point away at Bradford City. The following season he scooped the Player of the Year award and played in all but one of the games as the Fourth Division title was won in 1970–71.

Nicknamed 'Neddy' he, along with 'Stubbsy', famously saved the Main Stand from burning down when they noticed smoke coming from one of the drying rooms. The pair saved Notts on many other occasions in more orthodox fashion!

After a second promotion in three years, Notts found themselves in the old Second Division, initiating the return of the Nottingham derby. Appropriately, it was a home match against Forest in March 1975 that brought up the milestone of County's 3,000th League match. That match was undoubtedly one of the highlights of the big defender's time at the club, as was the League Cup win at Leeds United a year later.

Around that period David was playing with the most consistent form of his career. Mercifully clear of injuries, he played in every League game from March 1974 to November 1977. There were always rumours that clubs were enquiring as to his availability, but they were always knocked back by the club, the player – or usually both!

Finally, though, David was allowed to leave to pursue a dream of playing in the top flight. He moved to QPR, after being given a testimonial by the Magpies. After just four months at Loftus Road, David was back in Nottingham, brought 'home' by Brian Clough. Even County fans looked on with a certain amount of respect as David ended his career on a high. Although he was often used as a squad player, he was very much involved as Forest won a League title, two European Cups and a couple of League Cups.

After making 86 League appearances for the Reds, he left in the summer of 1982 to play for Toronto Blizzard in Major League Soccer. His return to the English game came at Kettering Town, where he spent three years as player-manager before eventually retiring to concentrate on his business interests.

David is actively involved with the Ex-Notts County Players Association, helping to organise fundraising events and reunion dinners. He remains part of the Magpies' folklore and is a frequent and welcome visitor to Meadow Lane.

Jon Nixon

Date of birth: 20 January 1948, Ilkeston, Derbyshire

Notts County record:

Appearances: League 179, FA Cup 12, League Cup 8, Others 0

Goals: League 32, FA Cup 3, League Cup 3, Others 0

Debut: 10 January 1970 v Exeter City (a) drew 1–1

Also played for: Ilkeston Town, Long Eaton United, Peterborough United, Shrewsbury Town, Barnsley, Halifax Town, Burton Albion, Grantham Town, Shepshed Charterhouse

In those pre-match debates about Notts County's greatest-ever winger there will be plenty of fans willing to nominate Jon Nixon as their all-time favourite. Yet 'Nico' did not even like the position. 'I hated playing there', he admits. 'I always wanted to be the centre-forward but they wouldn't let me!'

He has special reason, therefore, for nominating his favourite playing partner. 'I loved being in the same side as Kevin Randall because he would occasionally ask to switch, as he liked a run on the flank – the trouble was I'd never let him switch back!'

Jon's route into the professional game was a tough one. Released as a youngster by Derby County – 'I'm sure they sent the letter to the wrong person' – he went to teacher training college to pursue another career. A Midland League title with Ilkeston Town and a stint at Long Eaton followed before he wrote to Notts County asking for a trial.

'Out of the blue I received a phone call from Tommy Lawton, who was the chief scout. They gave me 10 minutes in a reserve match. I ran around like a headless chicken but didn't even touch the ball. I thought my chance had gone but they asked me back. This time I played against Mansfield Town, scored a cracker and was taken on.'

His debut came away at Exeter City, one of just nine appearances in the latter part of the 1969–70 season. The following year he played in every game bar one, as Notts cruised to the Fourth Division title. 'We had a great team that season. My job was so easy because of Don Masson. Every time I set off on a run, the ball would be delivered, inch-perfect, straight to my feet. He really was a marvellous player.'

That year Jon scored his most memorable goal in a Notts jersey. 'It was at home against Northampton Town and it was Tony Hateley's homecoming game. Over 21,000 were in Meadow Lane and I scored the only goal. A ball came in from the left, was touched at the near post and I struck a volley from the edge of the box that whistled into the net.'

An ever-present in the 1971–72 season, Jon suddenly found his goalscoring boots the following year, with 17 goals in the League and another in the cup. 'After Christmas I just couldn't stop scoring. I've still got a press cutting somewhere that said that Bill Nicholson was interested in taking me to Spurs. Jimmy Sirrel saw it and remarked, "They're nae 'avin' you. You're nae goin' anywhere!" '

Jon eventually did move on, with Noel Cantwell smashing Peterborough's transfer record to sign the winger. 'I'd loved my time at Notts but the time was right. The club felt they could make a bit of money and Steve Carter and Ian Scanlon were just coming through.'

After doing the rounds of several League and non-League clubs Jon hung up his boots after a return to Meadow Lane. 'I played for the ex-Notts County side against a team of ex-Forest players. Throughout my career I'd only ever had a broken nose and a broken collar bone but in this "friendly" I severed my Achilles tendon. What a way to end your career!'

'Nico' lives in West Hallam, Notts, and works as a Sales Manager for an auto print company in Sandhurst. He still recalls, with fondness, those happy days as a Magpie. 'I was fortunate that I had a little bit of pace – they used to say "open the gates, here he comes!" From time to time I still look at my championship medal and remember some really wonderful times.'

Stefan Oakes

Date of birth: 6 September 1978, Leicester

Notts County record:

Appearances: League 44, FA Cup 3, League Cup 1, Others 0

Goals: League 5, FA Cup 1, League Cup 0, Others 0

Debut: 21 February 2004 v Stockport County (h) won 4–1

Also played for: Leicester City, Crewe Alexandra, Walsall, Wycombe Wanderers

In the clubs and pubs of Nottingham, for many years to come, there will be those fortunate enough to say, 'I was there'.

County fans, habitually accustomed to disappointment, feared the worst. Four defeats on the bounce and a never-ending journey to Somerset to face League leaders Yeovil Town. Throw in a wet, drizzly evening and the outcome seemed inevitable, but sometimes football surprises you and so it was on Tuesday 29 March 2005 at Huish Park. The game, just five minutes old – step forward Stefan Oakes.

The midfielder had arrived at Meadow Lane early in 2004. Great things were expected, even though he arrived after serving a ban for a sending-off for Walsall, his only start for the club. Stefan's career was at the crossroads after 64 League appearances for Leicester City, his hometown club, then a loan spell at Crewe and a free transfer to Walsall. In seven months he failed to establish himself at the Bescot Stadium, so was more than happy to sign for Notts, shortly after Gary Mills took over as manager.

In the final 14 matches of the 2003–04 season, Stefan showed himself to be an accurate distributor of the ball but, despite possessing a powerful shot, he failed to open his goal account for his new club.

Stefan explained his shoot-on-sight theory. 'I'm very rarely around the six-yard box to score tap-ins, so it's usually a long-range effort. If I get space I'll hit it from anywhere. Most of the time they end up in the stand but if you don't shoot, you don't score.'

His first goal for the Magpies came at Swindon in the FA Cup – a typically lashed drive that arrowed its way towards its intended target. League goals at Grimsby and Wycombe then followed, with the latter a real stunner, a 35-yarder that flew into the top corner, with the 'keeper groping at fresh air.

So Stefan's goal tally stood at three for the season when he lined up at Yeovil. Notts in their all sky-blue away strip lay 20th in the table and feared a real beating.

There was little indication of any danger when Oakes picked up the ball near to the halfway line. He advanced forward and from all of 45 yards he hit the ball with all the pace and accuracy he could muster. The trajectory was perfect. Despite goalkeeper Chris Weale back-peddling for all he was worth he could not lay a glove on the ball and Notts were sensationally ahead.

The official away attendance in the 7,221 crowd was just 250 but they made the noise of 10 times that amount in jubilation at what they had seen. Notts went on to win the match 3–1, thereby winning the League Managers Association's Performance of the Week award.

The long journey home was spent debating over whether it was the finest County goal of all time. Stefan himself answered that one. 'I would probably say my Wycombe one was even better!'

Ironically, Oakes left Notts in the summer of 2005 to join Wycombe Wanderers, but he will always be remembered at Meadow Lane for his explosive long-range shooting and his fabulous wonder goal.

Ray O'Brien

Date of birth: 21 May 1951, Dublin

Notts County record:

Appearances: League 323, FA Cup 11, League Cup 24, Others 27
Goals: League 31, FA Cup 0, League Cup 4, Others 4
Debut: 16 March 1974 v Preston North End (a) won 2–0

Also played for: Shelbourne, Manchester United, Boston United, Republic of Ireland (5 caps)
Managed: Boston United, Corby Town, Arnold Town

There have not been that many players who could strike a dead-ball as well as Ray O'Brien. The Irish left-back became a master of the set-piece during his nine years at Notts and fans still recall some of his net-bursting free kicks and penalties.

Ray was one of eight children and two of his brothers, Fran and Derek, also played football professionally but he nearly missed out because his father would not let him sign for Torquay United, for whom he had impressed in a trial. 'I'd gone over there and manager Frank O'Farrell was interested in offering me an apprenticeship. My father insisted I had to get a trade behind me, so I became an apprentice printer.'

Playing for Shelbourne in the League of Ireland, Ray continued to turn in good performances and O'Farrell had not forgotten him. 'Frank had become Manchester United manager and was still keen to sign me. Before the deal could go through, he was replaced by Tommy Docherty. The Doc and Paddy Crerand came over and watched me, and fortunately I was soon on my way to Old Trafford.'

Ray spent a year at United without making a single first-team appearance. He was informed that Notts County had made an enquiry about his availability. 'My immediate reaction was that I didn't want to leave but the more I thought about it, the more I wanted first-team football.'

The transfer went through, with Notts paying £45,000, a club record at the time. First impressions were good. 'I was shocked by the standard of player at Notts County. I hadn't seen anyone at United as good as Don Masson!'

Manager Jimmy Sirrel spent an eternity converting Ray into a dead-ball specialist. 'He had a board specially made to the exact specification of a four-man 'wall' and it used to be wheeled on to the car park every day for my benefit.' The day of reckoning arrived in November 1974 when Hull City visited Meadow Lane. Notts were awarded a free-kick on the edge of the box. 'I remember Masson saying, "You can do it." I hit it true enough and the ball flew in. All that practice had paid off.'

Over the next seven or eight years the sight of Ray lining up for a blast at goal was a common spectacle for County fans. He also took the responsibility of converting penalties and had a particularly successful time in the 1979–80 season. Thanks to seven spot-kicks he totalled 10 goals in all to finish as the club's top scorer.

By then Ray had fulfilled an outstanding ambition by playing international football for his country. 'My best game was in Poland when I marked Lato and we won 2–0.' His fifth and final appearance for the Republic came against World Champions Argentina, when he was brought on as a substitute to play in midfield. 'People say I got a close look at Maradona – but to be honest I didn't really get that close to him!'

In 1984, Ray was awarded a testimonial by Notts County, with Sheffield Wednesday providing the opposition. Shortly afterwards he moved into the non-League game, linking up with a former teammate, Arthur Mann, at Boston United. Ray succeeded Arthur as manager of the Pilgrims and also had spells in charge at Corby Town and Arnold Town before putting his early training to good use by becoming a director of a printing company.

Living in Beckingham, near Newark, Ray still follows the fortunes of the Magpies and is an immensely popular figure whenever he returns to Meadow Lane.

James Oswald

Date of birth: 3 January 1868, Greenock

Died: 26 February 1948

Notts County record:

Appearances: League 95, FA Cup 11, Others 1

Goals: League 55, FA Cup 9, Others 0

Debut: 7 September 1889 v Wolverhampton Wanderers (a) lost 0–2

Also played for: Third Lanark, St Bernards, Glasgow Rangers, Scotland (3 caps)

It was considered quite a coup for Notts when they signed Scottish international James 'Jimmy' Oswald, in time for the start of the 1889–90 season. More so, it seemed, when he persuaded his younger brother Johnny, a Third Lanark teammate, to join him in Nottingham. Alas, Johnny's contribution was minimal and after just one season his offer to remain at the club was declined by the Board of Directors. Jimmy, though, was an unheralded success. The Scot top-scored in each of the four seasons he was with the club, a spell which yielded five hat-tricks; four in the League and one in the FA Cup.

Short of stature, at around 5ft 6in tall, his assets were immense strength, a vicious shot and a striker's instinct to sniff out a half-chance. Vocal on and off the pitch and well respected by his colleagues, Jimmy was a natural leader. He would be prepared to sweat blood for the cause and expected the same commitment from those around him.

His first season with the Magpies yielded 15 goals from 19 Division One appearances. The season after, his tally was 14 in the League, the major contribution in a third-place finish. As good as the League campaign had been, it was the FA Cup competition of 1890–91 that was particularly memorable for Notts County, as they reached the final for the first time. Along the way they had defeated Sheffield United, Burnley, Stoke City and Sunderland helped, to a large degree, by five goals from Oswald, including both in the 2–0 semi-final replay win over the team from Wearside.

On the big day itself, the opponents were Blackburn Rovers. The match was to be played in London at the Kennington Oval and Notts were overwhelming favourites. A huge contingent of the 23,000 present had travelled down from Nottingham but it was a journey that witnessed a crushing defeat.

Just seven days earlier County had gone to Blackburn and triumphed 7–1 in a League match, with Jimmy helping himself to two of the goals. As captain and top scorer, much was expected of Jimmy at the Oval. Despite his enthusiasm and will-to-win, Notts were poor in the first half and leaked three goals. The manner of Jimmy's 70th minute consolation was not recorded – suffice to say it was a disappointed side that made their way home.

Jimmy scored 15 goals the following season but a downward slide had begun and the 1892–93 season resulted in relegation. Their main striker notched just 11 goals – three of them coming in an 8–1 thrashing of West Bromwich Albion.

With the expected loss of revenue from their drop into Division Two, Notts were facing a cash crisis. Club accounts record that Jimmy was on extremely good terms at Notts, with a salary documented at £175 per year – way above the national average. Spending above their means, some players had to renegotiate their contracts. Jimmy was not happy and refused to accept reduced terms. He returned to Scotland and ended up at Glasgow Rangers. However, before that Jimmy did taste some cup success. Playing for the now-defunct Edinburgh side St Bernard's, he appeared in their 1895 Scottish Cup final-winning side. The Saints defeated Renton by two goals to one in a match played at Ibrox.

Notts County's first FA Cup final captain at last had a winners' medal.

Charlie Palmer

Date of birth: 10 July 1963, Aylesbury

Notts County record:

Appearances: League 182, FA Cup 10, League Cup 9, Others 20

Goals: League 7, FA Cup 0, League Cup 0, Others 2

Debut: 18 February 1989 v Chester City (a) lost 0–1

Also played for: Watford, Derby County, Hull City, Walsall, Burton Albion, Moor Green, Hinckley United

Although Charlie Palmer played in 182 League matches for Notts County, his other achievements tend to be overshadowed by the events of 12 February 1994 – derby day. For too long, the red half of the city's football culture had held sway – but this was Notts' day. The day 'Sir Charlie Palmer' had his finest moment. 'In spite of everything I achieved in my football career, fans only remember me because of that goal. More than 10 years on, I'm still asked about it.'

Notts had relinquished the lead, given to them through Gary McSwegan, when Dave Phillips scored an 85th minute equaliser for Forest. Less than 60 seconds later, Charlie entered County folklore.

'We had a free kick on the left. I'm not sure what happened to start with but the referee blew straight away for it to be retaken. I turned and walked back and signalled for Mark Draper to hit it deep. His right peg hit an unbelievable ball – I made my run and got above Stuart Pearce to head it in. I've got to admit I lost it at that point – I just went wild with emotion.'

Apart from his frenzied goal celebration, Charlie has another memory of that day. 'I just had a quiet drink with my wife that night, while everyone else went out and partied. Given the effect it had, perhaps we should have gone out on the town as well.'

Aside from his unforgettable individual contribution for Notts, Charlie should also be remembered for his role in the two Wembley play-off wins. 'I didn't get any sleep before the Tranmere match', he recalls. 'Everyone told me to take the occasion on board and not let it pass me by. It did, of course, but the following year I knew what to expect and was able to enjoy what we'd done.'

Charlie was a tough-tackling, no-nonsense defender who had graduated through the ranks from apprentice to the first team at Watford before enjoying spells at Derby County and Hull City. Neil Warnock signed him for Notts for £25,000 in 1989. 'He was a very good manager, able to get the most out of what he'd got. He looked for players who were hungry to achieve success and blended us into a very good side indeed.'

After six years at Meadow Lane, Charlie joined Walsall before entering the non-League game with Burton Albion and then Hinckley United. At the latter he linked up with ex-Notts colleague Dean Thomas, who persuaded Charlie to move into coaching. 'Anybody who knew me a few years ago would be staggered that I turned to coaching, but Dean gave me a chance and I've enjoyed the experience. He's taught me so much and I'd like to think I'm able to add something to our working relationship. The good thing is, we've made progress every year.'

To complete a very full and demanding life, Charlie works as a social worker. 'I'm mainly involved with under-privileged kids and try to pass on some of my experience. They know that I played football and most are prepared to listen to me and talk to me. I tell them that I came from a working-class background and went on to fulfil most of my ambitions. If I'm able to help any of them at all – then I'm doing my job.'

Derek Pavis

Date of birth: 12 March 1930, Nottingham

Notts County record:
Chairman: 1987–2002
Life President: 2002–

Like all true, honest, straight-talking people Derek Pavis has had his critics. Some Notts County fans will be amongst them but for the vast majority he will be regarded as the saviour of the club, the man who spent vast sums of his own wealth to keep the Magpies from going under.

Nottingham born and bred, he was denied the opportunity to become chairman at Nottingham Forest when he was voted off the board of directors, while serving as the vice-chairman. 'There was a rotation system in which the vice-chairman would naturally succeed the chairman', explains Derek. 'They knew I'd been the only one to stand up to Brian Clough about his expenditure. I think they were a little worried in case Brian walked out if I got in, so they voted me out.' Hurt by the decision, Derek had a year away from football. 'I would take the wife shopping on Saturday afternoons instead – so I was really scraping the barrel!' he laughs.

With his own businesses on the up and up, Derek considered a return to the game and was in talks with a number of clubs when he received a telephone call. 'John Mounteney told me that Jack Dunnett might be interested in selling up.' Possibly the most remarkable negotiations in history then took place. 'After a number of discussions we got together in the offices of Wells and Hind solicitors and talked and talked for 19 hours! We eventually broke up at 4am with the deal done. I went home and rang a number of people, then went to the ground at nine o'clock. I have to admit my first thoughts were "What have I done?" '

The new chairman immediately brought in the experienced John Barnwell as manager, the first in a long line to serve under Mr Pavis. 'It's easy to say that Neil Warnock and Sam Allardyce were the best two because of what they achieved but I have to say I'm proud of the way young managers like Russell Slade, Gary Brazil and Mick Walker went about their business. They each impressed me in certain ways.'

Not all appointments lived up to expectations. Derek admits the acquisition of one particular manager was a mistake. 'For a number of reasons Howard Kendall wasn't the right man for the job. However, I wasn't around to make a decision about his future as I'd gone to Spain and had been taken poorly. They admitted me into intensive care with an abscess on my colon. I knew nothing about it but when I came round a couple of days later I learned that the board had sacked him in my absence.'

Derek is justifiably happy to recall the happier times of his reign. 'To have gone to Wembley five times under my stewardship makes me very proud. The second of the play-off finals is possibly the biggest highlight. After beating Brighton, I ran on to the Wembley pitch and hugged Neil Warnock and Mick Jones and heard 28,000 Notts fans singing, "There's only one Derek Pavis". A few months later I saw some "Pavis Out" banners at Meadow Lane – I suppose that's football!'

Apart from success on the playing side Derek takes immense pleasure every time he surveys the stadium at Meadow Lane. 'We built four new stands in just 17 weeks for a total outlay of only £8 million', he reveals. 'Craig Short and Tommy Johnson went to Derby for £5 million, we got another two from a Football Trust grant, half a million from the council and I put half a million in myself. I won't be around in 50 years time but I think most of those stands will be!'

When Albert Scardino took over as Notts chairman in 2002, Derek was appointed as Life President in recognition of all he had achieved. His other lasting legacy is the Main Stand at Meadow Lane, which is now called 'The Derek Pavis Stand' in his honour.

Kevin Randall

Date of birth: 20 August 1945, Ashton-under-Lyne, Lancashire

Notts County record:

Appearances: League 121, FA Cup 7, League Cup 7, Others 0

Goals: League 39, FA Cup 4, League Cup 4, Others 0

Debut: 16 August 1972 v York City (h) won 3–1 (League Cup)

Also played for: Bury, Chesterfield, Mansfield Town, York City, Alfreton Town, Goole Town

Managed: York City, Chesterfield

Kevin Randall was already a proven goalscorer by the time he arrived at Meadow Lane and he wasted no time in getting off the mark for his new club, with a goal on his debut against York City.

Jimmy Sirrel had urged his board to fund the signing of Kevin, promising them promotion if they backed him. 'I'll always be grateful to Jimmy', says the former County striker. 'He stuck his neck out for me and in the end it paid off.'

The season did not begin well though, according to Kevin. 'We were something like sixth from bottom at Christmas and going nowhere. Then we beat Watford and drew at Bolton and it kicked our season into life.' With 23 goals Kevin finished as the Magpies' leading marksman, including two on the final day. 'We had to beat Tranmere to go up and hammered them 4–1. Everyone went out for dinner and Jimmy stood up and said some nice things about me, which was the last thing I needed with all the other players there, ready to take the mickey!'

Lancashire-born, Kevin might well have spent a lucrative career as a Manchester United player. His schools football had been spent playing for Droylsden and Ashton-under-Lyne and he was invited to Old Trafford for training. He played for United's junior side and made several appearances at 'B' team level.

Despite this, he grew up as a Manchester City fan, with Denis Law his favourite player. In his book *Steak Diana Ross*, David McVay mocked Kevin for not having the courage to ask Law for his autograph when he met him. 'He made up for it later though', laughs Kevin. 'He actually got me a signed photo of Denis.' It was also McVay who revealed Kevin's nickname to the world. 'They used to call me "The Claw". It started at Chesterfield and is quite complimentary I suppose. They reckoned I would push the ball beyond a defender, then "claw" my way round him!'

Kevin's first taste of League football came at Bury but after just eight months at Gigg Lane he moved to Chesterfield. During a six-year stay at Saltergate, Kevin scored over a century of goals from almost 300 outings. His strike partnership with Ernie Moss was among the most feared in the lower leagues.

During his three-year stay with Notts, Kevin scored at an average of a goal every three matches and is particularly fond of a couple of them. 'Probably my best goal for the club was against Portsmouth in the FA Cup. I chased it out wide, cut inside, beat the marker and smashed a fierce shot past the 'keeper.' His other favourite was a late equaliser as County came back from 2–0 down to draw with Manchester United. 'As a City fan I really enjoyed that, particularly as I had to go back to Manchester that night to a presentation evening!'

The striker moved on to enjoy stints at Mansfield Town and York City, where he also had a spell as caretaker manager. After short periods in and out of the non-League game, and a brief stint back at Chesterfield as manager, Kevin returned to Mansfield as part of the backroom staff. He then went back to Saltergate as assistant to John Duncan before joining the staff at Sheffield United, initially on the coaching side but latterly as chief scout.

Associated with several clubs throughout his time in football, Kevin regards his days at Meadow Lane as amongst the happiest. 'My wife and I used to enjoy popping in the Centenary Club. Everybody was just so friendly towards us. I'll never be able to thank Jimmy enough for signing me and I still keep in touch with Jack Wheeler, who is one of the nicest men I've ever met.'

Dave Regis

Date of birth: 3 March 1964, Paddington

Notts County record:

Appearances: League 56, FA Cup 15, League Cup 2, Others 6

Goals: League 17, FA Cup 0, League Cup 0, Others 2

Debut: 29 September 1990 v Bristol Rovers (h) won 3–2

Also played for: Barnet, Plymouth Argyle, Bournemouth, Stoke City, Birmingham City, Southend United, Barnsley, Peterborough United, Scunthorpe United, Leyton Orient, Lincoln City

As all good strikers will confirm, 'It doesn't matter how you put it there, so long as you put it in the net!'

Although it was neither the prettiest nor the most high-profile goal ever scored at Wembley Stadium, Dave Regis and the Magpies fans could not care. Neil Warnock's side were looking for their second consecutive play-off final win and Brighton and Hove Albion would not lie down and be beaten until Dave made the game safe with County's third. 'It was a free-kick out on the right. I took up a position where I could attack the ball at the far post. As it came in I got in front of my marker but the ball was too low to head. It hit me hard on the chest and flew in past the keeper.' That goal was the icing on the cake and sealed County's 3–1 win and promotion back into the top flight.

Having joined Notts at the start of the season from Barnet, it had been a rapid rise up the football ladder for the powerfully-built forward. From junior football he had gone straight into Barnet's first team and his 16 goals helped the side to the championship and a place in the Football League. Although under pressure to sell, manager Barry Fry was thought to be reluctant to part with any of his players, but his board accepted Notts County's bid for Dave and teammate Paul Harding.

Used mainly as a substitute in the first part of the season, Dave was given time to adjust to the pace of life at County. His first goal came after leaving the bench, away at Oldham Athletic.

During November 1990 manager Neil Warnock began to play Dave from the start and the decision reaped huge dividends. With 15 goals in the League, Regis finished just one behind top scorer, Tommy Johnson. Amongst Dave's haul was three in the home win over Plymouth Argyle on 27 April 1991, his first senior hat-trick.

When Notts County marked their return to the top flight, away at Manchester United in August 1991, Dave was included in the side and given the opportunity to impress at the highest level. Whether his physical game would have succeeded against the very best defenders is open to conjecture because after just nine appearances the Magpies received a bid of £200,000 from Plymouth Argyle for him. Clearly the Devon side had been very impressed by what he had done to them at Meadow Lane.

Dave then began to change clubs with alarming frequency – moving about in search of the right location. For a while he teamed up again with Barry Fry, at Birmingham City, but the stay was brief – as it became at many other clubs.

In February 1997, while on the books of Barnsley, Dave returned to Meadow Lane on loan. He made an immediate impact, scoring on his 'second' debut – away at Shrewsbury. Another goal came against Rotherham United but the move did not become permanent and the player returned to Oakwell.

After his playing days were over Dave settled in Nottingham and pulled on the black and white stripes again, when he represented the Magpies in the Masters football tournament in the summer of 2005.

Although he became something of a footballing nomad later in his career, Dave Regis will always be remembered by the fans of Notts County – especially for that goal at Wembley.

Pedro Richards

Date of birth:　　11 November 1956, Edmonton, North London
Died:　　　　　　23 December 2001

Notts County record:
Appearances:　　League 399, FA Cup 19, League Cup 38, Others 28
Goals:　　　　　League 5, FA Cup 0, League Cup 1, Others 0
Debut:　　　　　23 November 1974 v Sunderland (a) lost 0–3

Also played for: Boston United, Oakham United, Corby Town

Just one more – that is all it would have taken for Pedro Richards to clock up 400 League appearances for the Magpies. Such was his consistency that he was a near ever-present for almost a decade and clocked up over 450 appearances in the famous stripes. Many critics were forced to admit that Pedro showed his real quality once Notts had reached the top flight and felt his three years in Division One were the best of his career.

Although most supporters would have assumed that the defender had taken a regular route into the professional game, it is not stretching the truth to state that Pedro had an unorthodox upbringing. Maria, his Spanish mother, came over to London to work and send money home for the rest of the family. She fell pregnant with Pedro and it was agreed that the child would be brought up in Spain by his grandparents.

For the first 12 years of his life Pedro lived in La Guardia, a small village near to Logrones in the north of the country. Naturally he could speak only Spanish, so it was a culture shock when his mother married and brought him back to England to live in the Meadows area of Nottingham. Pedro attended the Roland Green School and, wonderfully athletic, he began to excel at football. So rapid was his development that he was taken on as an apprentice by County, at just 15 years of age.

Many judges felt he was destined to go right to the very top of the game and certainly he was regarded, at that age, as a better prospect than Viv Anderson, a fellow Nottingham schoolboy who went on to such outstanding success at international level.

David McVay, a teammate of Pedro's, explains how he spurned his big opportunity. 'He was invited to one England call-up at Lilleshall for an Under-20 or 21 get-together but he didn't want to go. He could be stubborn over things like that and the authorities didn't take to being rebuffed. I also think Pedro felt he was probably more Spanish than English anyway!'

Pedro 'real name Peter' enjoyed a seven-match run at left-back during the 1974–75 season, filling in for Ray O'Brien. His potential was obvious – more so the year after when he became established at right-back.

The Richards' era had begun in earnest as he cemented a place in the side with honest, hard-working commitment and consistency. Cheery and likeable, Pedro was admired by the fans and respected by his colleagues.

He enjoyed his football – never more so than on 30 April 1977, when he scored his first Notts goal at home to Southampton. Then, as he did most summers, he would depart to spend the close season back in Spain. One summer he had a surprise visitor, as David McVay reveals. 'Without telling him I drove out to Spain, intending just to call in and say hello. It was a beautiful, picturesque village and I ended up staying for three idyllic weeks. They had a bull run there – rather like Pamplona – and to see Pedro happy and relaxed in his own environment is how I'll always remember him.'

The emergence of Tristan Benjamin enabled Jimmy Sirrel to switch Pedro to sweeper. The move was inspirational as Notts clinched their promotion to the old Division One. Playing against the best in the land suited the competitiveness of Pedro – it says much about the quality of those around him that he had to wait until the team had been relegated before he claimed his only Player of the Year award from the supporters.

After leaving Notts, Pedro spent a couple of enjoyable seasons with Boston United before continuing on the non-League circuit with spells at Oakham United and Corby Town.

Sadly, the man who used to be idolised by supporters in his prime became something of a recluse in his retirement. Believed to be living the life of a vagrant he contracted pneumonia in the latter part of 2001. Reluctant to seek proper treatment, he died at the tragically premature age of just 45.

Ian Richardson

Date of birth: 22 October 1970, Bolton

Notts County record (to end of season 2004–05):
Appearances: League 253, FA Cup 20, League Cup 18, Others 6
Goals: League 21, FA Cup 2, League Cup 2, Others 1
Debut: 20 January 1996 v Wrexham (h) won 1–0

Manager: November 2004–May 2005
Also played for: Dagenham and Redbridge, Birmingham City

Those that question whether there is any loyalty left in professional football need only look at the example provided by Ian Richardson. Although he was born in Lancashire, played non-League in Essex and made his League debut for Birmingham City, you will struggle to find anyone who cares more about Notts County Football Club.

During the darkest days of the club's administration Ian refused to contemplate the Magpies' glorious history reaching an inglorious conclusion. 'Believe me, it was a worrying time for everybody', he admits. 'No one really knew if you were going to get paid or not, or whether you'd be sold against your wishes. There were a few people that were prepared to sit back and let nature take its course but I wanted to do more than that.'

Known as 'Ricco' or 'Richo' to his many friends in the game, the long-serving defender was a leading fundraiser in the fight to keep County afloat – and help was not very far away. 'One morning my wife, Debbie, said she was going to try and raise some money. She just went off with a bucket and stood outside the ASDA supermarket all day asking for donations for the club. I'm pleased to say that she did very well!'

Apart from spontaneous bucket collections, Ian knows that the club owes a debt of thanks to many people who showed how much they care. 'The Supporters Trust were simply fantastic in all their fundraising efforts. Together with a donation from a mystery backer and the money raised from the Chelsea cup match the club managed to survive.'

Ian was playing as a central midfielder when he made his debut for Notts County during a brief loan move, but he was recalled by Birmingham City to play in a League Cup semi-final. Although the St Andrews' side offered him a new contract, he had enjoyed his time at Meadow Lane and was happy to sign on a permanent deal. 'I just wanted to play football and thought my chances at Birmingham would be restricted. Notts paid £200,000 for me, so I hope I've given them good value!'

That 1995–96 season saw Notts reach the play-off final at Wembley Stadium but a 2–0 defeat to Bradford City spoilt the occasion. 'It's everyone's dream to play there and the atmosphere was brilliant but the occasion got to a lot of people and we felt very disappointed about the way we performed.'

During the period under Sam Allardyce, 'Ricco' was finally converted into a central defender, though he reveals he had played there before. 'I'd played in that position for Dagenham and in the Anglo-Italian tournament for Birmingham, so it wasn't totally true that Sam was responsible for the switch.'

Nevertheless, the 1997–98 season, in which Ian starred in defence, was one of the club's finest in living memory. Records were smashed as County romped to the Third Division title. All too soon though, handicapped during the traumatic period of administration, the playing side went into freefall and again Notts found themselves in the bottom flight.

A disappointing start to the 2004–05 season contributed to Gary Mills leaving his post as County manager and the board turned to 'Ricco' to step in. 'They asked me to become caretaker until the end of the season. I went away and thought about it and decided to accept because the club means so much to me. I told the players that they were in the position they were in because they'd underachieved.'

Ian's problems as boss were compounded by his own absence through injury but he won 11 and drew 9 of the 34 matches in which he was in charge of the club. 'There was an initial indication that if I kept the club in the League then the job might be offered to me on a permanent basis but when they decided to go for someone with a little more experience I fully understood.'

As the 2005–06 season began Ian's aim was to carry on playing for as long as he could but his first taste of management had not put him off the job. Whether it has been as a player, manager or simply through raising money for the coffers, Ian Richardson's loyalty to Notts County will never be forgotten.

Norman Rigby

Date of birth: 23 May 1923, Warsop, Notts

Died: 21 August 2001

Notts County record:

Appearances: League 46, FA Cup 3

Goals: League 0, FA Cup 0

Debut: 15 April 1948 v Ipswich Town (h) lost 0–1

Also played for: Newark Town, Peterborough United

Managed: Peterborough United

Norman Rigby was not at Notts for long but was an integral part of the side that won the Division Three South championship in 1949–50.

He had joined a local side, Newark Town, as a promising youngster, but his football career was put on hold with the outbreak of war. His call-up preceded a lengthy spell of active service in India. Resuming his football, he was taken on by Notts and given a debut towards the end of the 1947–48 season, as stand-in for the regular left-back, Bert Howe. A one-goal defeat dented Norman's pride that day but he was soon establishing himself in the number three jersey.

A tall, strong defender, Norman Rigby was a winger's nightmare – a pacy full-back who rarely mistimed a tackle.

One person with special reason for recalling Rigby's time with Notts is Barry Lord, a lifelong County fan from Newark. 'As a young supporter I was fortunate that my family knew Norman', says Barry. 'He lived at 144 Trent Boulevard, Nottingham, next door to my aunt. Over a time I'd got to know him quite well and was delighted when he said he'd take me to the games with him. I would get on one of Gash's buses from Newark. My aunt would meet me on Radcliffe Road and then Norman would take me to the match. To witness that season was a delight for every County fan but for a youngster it was made even more special because I actually knew one of the players so well.'

Barry's friendship with Norman enabled him to meet the other County players of that era. 'After the matches most of the players would just say their goodbyes and leave as there was no such thing as a players' bar in those days. Often, though, I would be able to meet some of the other players and felt so proud to be introduced to the likes of Tommy Lawton and Jackie Sewell. With Norman's help I managed to get all of the autographs and a few other souvenirs which I still treasure to this day.'

While several of his teammates grabbed most of the headlines, Norman Rigby's contribution to the title success was immense – he was one of the true unsung heroes.

Times move on, especially in football, and in the following season Notts were particularly well blessed in the full-back department. Tommy Deans, Billy Corkhill and Aubrey Southwell were all staking their own claims for a jersey. As a result, Norman was often omitted and decided to move on.

After leaving Meadow Lane he went on to enjoy even greater success with Peterborough United. During their non-League reign, he helped them achieve five consecutive Midland League championship titles and, following their elevation to the Football League, he skippered them to the Fourth Division title at the first time of asking in the 1960–61 season.

In the late 1960s, Norman Rigby spent a couple of seasons as Peterborough's manager before retiring to Newark, where he passed away in 2001, aged 78.

Ian Scanlon

Date of birth: 13 July 1952, Stirling

Notts County record:

Appearances: League 111, FA Cup 1, League Cup 10, Others 9

Goals: League 31, FA Cup 0, League Cup 3, Others 1

Debut: 29 July 1972 v Sheffield United (h) lost 0–3 (Watney Cup)

Also played for: East Stirling, Aberdeen, St Mirren

'Super Scanny' was a terrace hero – the more the fans loved him, the more he responded. An enigma at times – you were never sure what you were going to get – he will always be remembered for an act of giant-killing and a three-goal blitz.

Ian Scanlon joined Notts in the summer of 1972 with a reputation for being a raw but willing wide player who had a keen eye for goal. His debut was fairly inauspicious, a home drubbing in the unfashionable Watney Cup competition. 'Scanny' kept his place for the opening match of a season, which was to end in promotion for County. Ian's involvement though was restricted to just four appearances, two of them as a substitute.

The following year was even bleaker, with just two outings. If anyone was beginning to doubt Jimmy Sirrel's wisdom in acquiring the young Scot, they were silenced in the 1974–75 season. Ian rose from oblivion to become top scorer, with 14 in the League. His first goal came at home to Leyton Orient on 24 September and he had only scored five by the time Sheffield Wednesday came to Meadow Lane on 16 November.

The Yorkshire side led 1–0 at the break, with no indication of the drama to unfold. Early in the second half, in the space of 2 minutes 45 seconds, Ian Scanlon scored three times, one of them from the penalty spot. Although Wednesday responded to earn a 3–3 draw, 'Scanny's' hat-trick entered the record books as the quickest ever scored by a Notts County player.

Later in the season, in another tense Meadow Lane encounter, Ian had the satisfaction of scoring against Nottingham Forest in another drawn contest – the match was Notts County's 3,000th League fixture.

Ian's best position was open to debate. He could certainly do a job out on the left wing, where he had the happy knack of being able to turn opposing full-backs inside out. For a while Notts had great width, with Ian on one side and Steve Carter on the other.

Many felt, though, that Ian was better playing down the middle, just to the left of centre. There, he scored some wonderful goals – but surely none as prestigious as his League Cup winner at Elland Road.

Leeds United had been England's most successful side in the early 1970s and had played in the European Cup final just five months before. County were given little chance when they kicked off a third-round tie on 8 October 1975. Somehow it remained scoreless until the break. Rather than hanging on for a draw the Magpies gave it their all. 'Scanny' missed a great chance and then hit a post. Les Bradd also went agonisingly near, but then the breakthrough came as Ian headed home. Have Notts ever pulled off a bigger cup shock?

The side were heroes – and the goalscorer even more so. Ian Scanlon's position in County's folklore was secured.

A lovely lad with a great left foot, his departure from Notts was bizarre in the extreme. Ian announced that he was quitting the game to marry a millionaire heiress. He later resurfaced in Scottish football to play for both Aberdeen and St Mirren.

Although his Football League career had been brief 'Super Scanny' certainly made his mark.

Jackie Sewell

Date of birth: 24 January 1927, Whitehaven, Cumberland

Notts County record:
Appearances: League 178, FA Cup 15
Goals: League 97, FA Cup 7
Debut: 14 September 1946 v Norwich City (h) won 3–0

Also played for: Kells Miners Welfare, Whitehaven Town, Sheffield Wednesday, Aston Villa, Hull City, England (6 caps)

There is no doubting that Jackie Sewell was one of the finest players ever to represent Notts County. That fact tends to be overlooked because he played alongside the great Tommy Lawton - but Jackie was a true star in his own right.

A wonderful athlete, with a keen eye for goal, he lies third in County's list of all-time League goalscorers, just behind Les Bradd and Tony Hateley, and remains one of the most popular figures ever to have represented the Magpies.

Although it is generally thought that Jackie first played for Notts during the 1946–47 season, he had actually 'guested' for the club in more than 20 wartime matches. His official League debut was a sign of things to come – a goal in a home victory over Norwich. That was the first of the 21 he scored that season as Jackie topped the scoring charts. The lack of a regular strike partner for him cost the side dearly, as they could only finish 12th in the Division Three South table.

In November 1947, Jackie scored the first of his five hat-tricks for County, all registered at Meadow Lane, when non-League Horsham were swept aside 9–1 in the FA Cup.

Jackie usually wore the number eight jersey, favouring the old-fashioned inside-forward position, rather than being the out-and-out striker.

Scoring goals in multiples became commonplace for the Notts attackers in 1948–49, Lawton's first full season at the club. A total of 68 League goals were scored at home, emphasised by some huge margins of victory. Jackie scored four of the goals when Newport County were defeated 11–1, the club's highest ever score in the Football League. He added another four in a 9–0 win over Exeter City and just one in a 9–2 victory over Ipswich Town. Staggeringly, Notts again contrived to finish in a lowly mid-table position. It was no consolation for Jackie that he was again the club's top marksman with 29 in all competitions.

Promotion did eventually arrive, but it was a couple of years behind schedule in most people's eyes. With three more matches remaining, Notts knew that a home victory over their city rivals on 22 April 1950 would ensure they went up. Jackie's 58th minute header from Tom Johnston's corner opened the scoring and when Tommy Lawton added a second it was a cue for the County fans to begin their celebrations.

Jackie continued to score regularly in Division Two, convincing any doubters that he could go all the way to the top. In March 1951, very much against the wishes of the fans, a bid from Sheffield Wednesday was accepted. It was no consolation that the British transfer record was broken, as the Owls parted with £34,500 to get their man – there was considerable unrest as County fans vented their displeasure at the board of directors.

Jackie left Meadow Lane having scored 97 League goals for the Magpies but continued to find the back of the net once he had switched to Hillsborough, scoring a total of 92 goals in 175 matches.

As so often happens, a high-profile move alerts the national selectors and, within eight months of leaving Notts, Jackie was called up for England for the first time.

His debut came in a 2–0 win over Northern Ireland, played at Villa Park. Although he went on to gain just six caps he scored three times – against Austria, Switzerland and Hungary – netting England's first in the notorious 3–6 home beating by the 'Magnificent Magyars'.

Jackie left Sheffield Wednesday in December 1955 to join Aston Villa and won an FA Cup winners' medal, helping them to a 2–0 victory over Manchester United in the 1957 final. His last move in English football was to Hull City, where he played for almost two seasons. Jackie then accepted an offer to go to Zambia, where he coached Lusaka City, before taking over a similar role with the national side.

After returning to Nottingham, Jackie became a car salesman but never lost his affection for the Magpies. He has continued to follow the club's fortunes throughout his retirement.

Craig Short

Date of birth: 25 June 1968, Bridlington, Yorkshire

Notts County record:
Appearances: League 128, FA Cup 8, League Cup 6, Others 16
Goals: League 6, FA Cup 1, League Cup 1, Others 2
Debut: 26 August 1989 v Blackpool (h) lost 0–1

Also played for: Pickering Town, Scarborough, Derby County, Everton, Blackburn Rovers, Sheffield United

In the mould of other famous Notts centre-halves of the past, Craig Short was tough as teak and a warm favourite with the fans. He proved to be a terrific asset when he moved to Meadow Lane for £100,000 in the summer of 1989. This was big money for the 'Pies, but the signing proved to be worth every penny, as Craig clocked up more than a century of League appearances, played in two successful promotion campaigns and eventually left for a club record transfer fee.

Having given up a fledgling career in the bank – 'I was supposed to be a trainee but I was the tea-boy really', he admits – Craig turned professional at Scarborough, who were newly promoted to the Football League under Neil Warnock. After his former boss took over at Notts County, Craig was offered the chance to follow him to Meadow Lane. 'I didn't have a great debut', he recalls. 'But I knew I'd joined a decent club. Dean Yates was great to play alongside, Tommy and Drapes were coming through, there was the experience with Phil Turner, Dean Thomas and Charlie Palmer, and Steve Cherry was a top class 'keeper.'

Craig's first campaign could not have ended any better. He played in all but two League matches and appeared in the play-off final success over Tranmere Rovers. 'We hadn't really shown ourselves to be genuine promotion contenders but picked up form at the right stage of the season and made it through to Wembley.' The night before the game the club's chairman handed over a gift and made a prophetic plea to the player. 'In the hotel Derek Pavis presented me with a framed photograph of me scoring against Cardiff City a few weeks earlier. "One of those tomorrow would be great", he said.'

Craig enjoyed his day beneath the Twin Towers. With Notts already leading 1–0 the tall defender experienced a moment he will always cherish. 'We'd worked on a free-kick routine where I spun away to the far post as a decoy. On this occasion Tommy Johnson overhit the kick and I was able to lose my marker and head it in. As I ran away celebrating I could see about 20 of my family and friends in the crowd. That made the moment even more special.'

During the subsequent close season younger brother Christian was also brought in from Scarborough and the pair appeared together for Notts on many occasions over the next couple of seasons.

To reach Wembley once was always regarded as a special moment in the career of any footballer but the Magpies made it there in consecutive years, reaching the play-off final at the end of the 1990–91 season. 'Strangely it wasn't as big a thing for me second time around', says Craig. 'I always thought we were going to win that one. The semi-final matches against Middlesbrough were far more tense. It would have been far more heartbreaking to lose at that stage.'

Having experienced success at two different clubs under Neil Warnock, Craig has nothing but admiration for his former boss. 'He engenders great team spirit and made training fun. You just didn't know what you were going to get with Neil – he was so innovative. I've gone in for training expecting a hard session and ended up going on a trip to the beach or taken for a walk in the dales. We also did things like spending the day on an army assault course or just simply eating bacon butties and talking. There was plenty of hard work too, of course, but he was a great bloke to work for.'

Justin Cast from Carlton is amongst the many Notts fans who believe that Craig is one of the finest defenders ever to play for the club. 'He never had a bad game for us and he forged a great partnership with Dean Yates. He had great speed, was good in the air and made many important last-ditch tackles. Above all, he was one of football's good guys.'

In September 1992, Craig played, and scored, in a midweek Anglo-Italian Cup-tie against Derby County – the following week he had joined the Rams for a staggering £2.5 million, the highest fee that Notts had ever received for a player.

'I think Notts were fortunate that two of the wealthiest chairmen around were interested in signing me. My valuation at that time should probably have been around £1.2 million but then Jack Walker, at Blackburn, and Lionel Pickering, at Derby County, both tried to sign me and the price became inflated. I actually went up to Blackburn and spoke to Kenny Dalglish but decided on Derby.' Ironically, after three years at Derby and then four at Everton, Craig did end up at Ewood Park and helped Rovers gain promotion back to the top flight. Craig joined Sheffield United for the 2005–06 season and was just a handful of matches away from completing the career milestone of 5,50 League appearances – not bad for the former bank trainee!

Jimmy Sirrel

Date of birth: 2 February 1922, Glasgow

Notts County record:

Manager: Three separate occasions (1969–75, 1978–82, 1985–87)

General Manager/Director: 1982–84

Also managed: Brentford, Sheffield United

Played for: Celtic, Bradford Park Avenue, Brighton and Hove Albion, Aldershot

During the 1960s the position of Notts County manager was not the most secure in League football. Frank Hill, Tim Coleman (twice), Eddie Lowe, Jack Burkitt, Andy Beattie and Billy Gray all held the post, as well as Jack Wheeler's 14-month stint in a caretaker capacity.

Stability was needed and it arrived in the form of a chirpy, confident Glaswegian who went on to transform the world's oldest club in the most remarkable fashion. 'Jack Dunnett invited me to become the Notts County manager', says Jimmy. 'He'd been my chairman at Brentford and he asked me to join him at Notts. I'd been quite impressed whenever I'd seen them play and thought they had some good young players, so I thought, "Why not?" '

The new boss soon began to organise his squad, with the help of his able lieutenant, the redoubtable Wheeler. 'Jackson [Jimmy's pet name for his loyal side-kick] was 1,000 percent committed to the club. No one could ask for anyone as hard working. We didn't need lots of coaches and assistants like they have in the modern game. I was the only one who addressed the players and Jackson dealt with the injuries and so on.'

Within 18 months Jimmy had led Notts to the Fourth Division title and the success continued with a further promotion just two years later. 'We were an underrated side. One rival manager at the time called us "The Land of the Giants" but we were better than that. We did have some big players but we had plenty of skilful, hardworking players as well. Above all else, we had winners.'

After steering County into Division Two for the first time since 1958, Jimmy stunned the Nottingham public by resigning to take over at Sheffield United. After a couple of seasons at Bramall Lane he returned to Meadow Lane to pick up where he left off. At the end of the 1980–81 season Notts were promoted to the top flight, the old Division One. Jimmy had completed the unique achievement of managing a side from Division Four into the top flight. 'The day at Chelsea, when promotion was confirmed, was the most marvellous occasion', he recalls. 'I did worry for my wife though, as she'd travelled down with the supporters and there were people running about everywhere after the game.'

In 1982, Howard Wilkinson stepped up from his role as coach to take over as manager, with Jimmy 'moving upstairs'. 'They found some fancy title for me – general manager, I think, and they made me a director of the club, which was nice.'

It was not the end of the Scot's managerial career, as he returned for a third stint at the club, but by now the 'Pies were back in Division Three. Jimmy eventually left Meadow Lane in May 1987 to become chief scout at Derby County but his legacy is there for all to see. 'Derek Pavis phoned me up one day and asked if they could name a stand after me. I said it would be a "bloody honour!" Hopefully it'll remain there for many, many years. It's really a wonderful accolade.'

Since retiring, Jimmy has continued to live at Burton Joyce, his home since moving to Notts in 1969. 'It's a lovely place to live – and it's just a few minutes from the ground so I can go back as often as I want.'

There will always be a warm reception at Meadow Lane for the manager who defied the odds and succeeded in taking Notts County from the bottom division into the top flight of English football.

Colin Slater

Date of birth: 28 February 1934, Shipley, West Yorkshire

Although he has never kicked a ball in anger in the professional game Colin Slater is, quite rightly, an integral part of Notts County's recent history. The 2004–05 season was his 46th reporting on the club's activities and his 37th doing so for BBC Radio Nottingham. It adds up to a staggering total of around 2,300 Notts matches, about 1,850 of them on radio.

Colin recalls the first time he set foot in Meadow Lane in 1959. 'I had just moved to Nottingham from Bradford to join the *Evening News* and *Football News* as both a general and a football reporter. Forest had just won the FA Cup but the paper's City Ground correspondent, the late Bryon Butler, had moved to Leicester, creating a vacancy. Editor Harry Swinburne thought the senior man, Albert Stapleton, should be switched from Notts to cover Forest and I should be assigned to Meadow Lane.'

So, on 22 August 1959, Colin covered his first Notts match – and witnessed a 2–1 home win over Chester in the old Fourth Division. As he recalls that was the start of a very successful season. 'Notts were promoted, finishing second in the table behind Walsall. However, instead of moving forward from there, Notts showed a lack of further ambition. I felt they had a useful squad of players which, with two or three additions, would have got the club back to Division Two.' The Magpies finished fifth, thirteenth and seventh before being relegated back to the Fourth Division in 1964.

Colin reflects on one of the club's poorer decisions. 'I feel the Board of Directors made a huge mistake in sacking manager Frank Hill in November 1961 and just as big an error of judgement in giving Eddie Lowe, Fulham's former England player, his first (and only) job in management. It was under him that Notts were relegated. The rest of the Sixties were awful as the club sank deeper.'

In fact Notts nearly sank out of existence. At a board meeting on 5 December 1965 the directors believed there was no option but to wind up the club's affairs. While in session they asked Colin to join them at the West Bridgford home of chairman Fred Williamson. Colin agreed to see the former Scotland and Forest manager, Andy Beattie, to ask if he would help, having been told that there was just a possibility of a new investor coming forward if he could be persuaded about the quality of the club's management.

Colin takes up the story. 'Andy and I were good friends but he did more than I ever expected. Not only did he agree to work at Meadow Lane as an unpaid advisor but he brought with him Peter Doherty, the former Northern Ireland manager. Together they formed such an impressive team that Bill Hopcroft, a local car dealer, immediately put £10,000 into the club, later became chairman – and Notts were saved. As I have often said, without Bill there would be no Jack Dunnett–Jimmy Sirrel era.'

Clearly Colin's involvement in helping to save the club remains at the forefront of his memories. 'My 46 seasons cover a long spell but I'm proudest of all of my role at that time, though I felt very privileged to be asked to front a night at the Astoria Ballroom in 1968. There, with 1,500 fans present, Lifeline was launched to inject much-needed extra funds into Notts.'

The Dunnett–Sirrel era did follow and, with the two of them at the helm, Notts climbed from the Fourth Division as champions in 1971 and in 1973 rose again to the Second Division. Eight years later, with Howard Wilkinson also on board, the journey to the top flight was achieved. 'The 2–0 win at Chelsea which ensured promotion to the First Division was one of the greatest occasions on which I've yet commentated', says Colin. Has there been anything to beat it? 'Yes, I think for sheer drama the successive play-off victories just have the edge, partly because of the setting of the old Wembley Stadium.'

Notts hit troubled waters again after slipping over a period of 13 seasons of decline in which they dropped back to the fourth tier (now Division Two) of the domestic game. Worst of all, it included an 18-month spell in administration, in which the club's future was once more in jeopardy.

Colin brushes lightly over his own involvement with the Blenheim Consortium and the Supporter's Trust, the combination that saved Notts but he says this: 'As my listeners may remember, I never lost faith. I simply could not believe that the oldest professional club in the world would be allowed to go under. I've witnessed many incredible moments following Notts but I'm not sure there's been anything to match the night of a dinner auction at Nottingham's Royal Hotel when the Trust reached its target of £250,000. It showed what can be achieved when everybody pulls together – directors, administrators, fans, players past and present – and if I might say so, the media as well. Is there a moral there somewhere?'

For almost half a century, to Magpies fans everywhere, Colin Slater has been 'the voice of Notts County'.

Aubrey Southwell

Date of birth: 21 August 1921, Grantham, Lincolnshire

Died: 9 February 2005

Notts County record:

Appearances: League 328, FA Cup 29

Goals: League 2, FA Cup 0

Debut: 19 October 1946 v Ipswich Town (h) lost 1–2

Also played for: Grantham Town, Nottingham Forest, Boston United

Aubrey Southwell was one of Notts County's longest serving full-backs. He clocked up over 350 first-team appearances after World War Two, remaining at Meadow Lane for more than a decade.

Born in Grantham, Aubrey attended the local Central School and played his first football with the junior club, Grantham St Johns. He then moved to the town's senior side, beginning the first of three spells with Grantham Town.

During the war Aubrey 'guested' for Notts County in more than 60 matches. Initially he played as a wing-half but was then converted into the back line, where he was to play for the rest of his career. Brief stints followed at Nottingham Forest and then back at Grantham before he rejoined the Magpies to begin a long and successful spell in the first team.

From making his full League debut, in October 1946, he did not miss a single fixture until injury forced him out of a match against Leyton Orient on 2 April 1949, a run of 120 games – 108 of them in the League. 'Mr Consistency' usually filled the right-back position during this phase of his career, with Bert Howe taking up his customary position on the left of the defence.

Ironically, Aubrey's most injury-prone season was 1949–50, which ended with Notts winning the Division Three South title. Despite long spells out, Aubrey still managed to clock up 18 League appearances and registered his first goal for the club in a 4–1 home win over Bristol City. The defender's only other strike came four years later against Swansea Town, also at home.

Apart from collecting his championship medal, Aubrey played in virtually all of Notts' major fixtures during the decade. He was a member of the side that defeated Newport County 11–1, the club's record League victory. He played in front of over 61,000 supporters in an FA Cup-tie at Liverpool, the largest attendance ever to watch a Notts County game. Aubrey also starred in the momentous FA Cup run in the 1954–55 season, when the side used the same 11 players for each match up until their sixth-round exit at the hands of York City.

Fittingly, Aubrey was appointed captain for his final season with the club and played his last game for Notts County on 23 February 1957 – a 2–2 home draw against Sheffield United. He moved to Boston United for the 1957–58 season, playing 37 times for the Pilgrims and notching up two goals – as many as he had scored in all his time at Notts. His final season in the game was spent back at Grantham.

Aubrey qualified as a practising physiotherapist but later became a salesman for a Nottingham-based brewery before becoming a wine merchant. Aubrey was always a keen golfer and spent much of his retirement relaxing on the golf course.

After a long illness Aubrey Southwell passed away in February 2005, aged 83.

Mark Stallard

Date of birth: 24 October 1974, Derby

Notts County record:

Appearances: League 201, FA Cup 10, League Cup 14, Others 2

Goals: League 69, FA Cup 3, League Cup 8, Others 0

Debut: 13 March 1999 v York City (h) won 4–2

Also played for: Derby County, Fulham, Bradford City, Preston North End, Wycombe Wanderers, Barnsley, Chesterfield, Shrewsbury Town

Mark Stallard twice won Notts County's Player of the Year award. The big striker served the club with distinction during one of its most difficult periods, and is delighted to have something tangible to look back on in years to come. 'Personally you can't get a higher accolade in the game than to be respected by your teammates and by the supporters. Every player likes to feel they contributed something at a club and to be voted for the award twice makes me feel very proud.'

With a total of 24 goals in season 2000–01 and 25 a couple of years later, Mark was perhaps a leading candidate to receive those awards but he feels there's more to his game than just sticking the ball in the net. 'Forwards tend to get judged by the amount of goals they score but sometimes that clouds the overall picture. I like to be able to drop off and hold the ball up for other players – you can't really do that if you are an out-and-out striker. I was fortunate at Notts that I usually played with Danny Allsopp or Paul Heffernan, both good players – but working as a pair helped my game.'

But for a double hernia operation, which forced him to miss three months of the 2001–02 season, he might have been on for a hat-trick of awards but he was pleased to recover so well from surgery. 'I was able to fire on all cylinders again and I think we played some decent football under Billy Dearden. Then things started to go wrong off the field.'

The club's financial plight has been well documented and Mark says the players were very aware of how serious it all became. 'There was definitely a time when there didn't seem to be a light at the end of the tunnel but the supporters were magnificent in everything they did to help save the club.'

Just when it was needed, the club were handed a plum draw in the League Cup – away against Chelsea. Although Mark scored in Notts' 4–2 defeat, the striker admits there were bigger issues at stake. 'The tie was a great opportunity for the club to make some money but the players deserve great credit for the way they performed. They put up a great show. We were all aware that those nights don't come along very often in a career and we were determined to make the most of it.'

Although 'Stal's goal that night was high profile, he does not rate it as his best goal for County. 'I scored one at home against Chesterfield – a lob from a tight angle. That's probably my favourite but I genuinely don't mind if it's from one yard or 20 so long as it goes in.'

Mark's transfer to Barnsley in January 2004 was regrettable, although understandable. 'It was a decision purely to reduce the wage bill – I didn't want to leave but knew it was inevitable; it was a business decision.' Times change – especially in football – and just over a year after leaving Meadow Lane, Mark was back in the black and white of Notts County, albeit on loan. 'I spoke to Ian Richardson and was happy to come back until the end of the season. We didn't pull up any trees but we had to ensure we pulled away from the bottom of the table and we did that.'

Mark's three-month loan spell allowed him to clock up a further 16 appearances, taking him beyond the 200 mark in League matches for Notts.

As the 2004–05 season drew to a close, Mark remained forthright on his views on the Magpies. 'There are about 85–90 clubs who believe they should be doing better but none have as much right as Notts County. They are a great club and I can't wait for the day when they are back where they belong!'

Brian Stubbs

Date of birth: 8 February 1950, Keyworth, Notts

Notts County record:
Appearances: League 426, FA Cup 22, League Cup 23, Other 16
Goals: League 21, FA Cup 1, League Cup 4, Other 1
Debut: 21 September 1968 v Swansea Town (h) lost 0–3

Also played for: Keyworth, Loughborough United, Grantham Town, Heanor Town

For over a decade opposing centre-forwards knew they were in for a tough ride when they played against Notts County. In an era of fully-committed individuals, Brian Stubbs was amongst the most fearless in the land – a six-foot plus, curly-haired warhorse – prepared to sweat blood for the cause. His partnership with another long-standing County player still evokes conversation. 'People always talk about me and Dave Needham but there were some other very good players who played for Notts County at that time. We had some decent quality all over the park.'

Those players have remained friends for over 30 years and it was a squad that played together, on and off the field. 'We all got on well together. Yes, we liked to socialise a bit but most of the time, even if we went for a drink, we would be talking football. Come three o'clock on a Saturday we were as committed as anyone – Jimmy Sirrel wouldn't have it any other way.'

It was not Jimmy, though, who gave 'Stubbsy' a surprise debut in the Magpies first team. 'Jack Wheeler was in charge as caretaker boss and was struggling for strikers, so he put me in and played me up front. I was pretty crap so he put me back to centre-half in the second half.'

The following season Brian really began to establish himself in the side, as much out of necessity as anything else. 'It was good money if you were playing, so that was all the incentive you needed to keep your form and fitness.'

Under Jimmy Sirrel, Notts lifted the Division Four title at the end of the 1970–71 season, and the supporters voted Brian as their Player of the Year. 'What a massive honour that was for me but it wasn't about individuals – we were a team, in the true meaning of the word. We all worked hard for each other and all had a job to do within the side.'

Renowned for his defensive abilities, Brian often proved himself to be a nuisance when he ventured upfield, chipping in with some important goals. 'The two I remember best were both set up by Don Masson. One was against Southampton – we broke quickly and Don crossed for me to power a flying header in from about 12 yards. The other was against Everton in the League Cup – I met a corner on the half-volley and it just flew in.'

Brian says he felt hard done by when he had to hand the club captaincy back to Masson. 'I lifted the Shipp Cup, County Cup and the Gibraltar Cup in the same season – then Don came back to the club and took over again – I must be the most successful captain ever to be sacked', he laughs.

Over the years there were many individual highlights – the League Cup win over Leeds United and tussles against some of the top strikers around stand out. 'Ted McDougall was a fierce competitor and Wolves' Derek Dougan and John Richards were as good a pairing as there was at that time.'

But for the famed defensive duo Notts might have needed a new Main Stand. 'Dave Needham and myself were in the treatment room one day – no one else was around. We could smell smoke and realised that a fire had started when a tea towel had fallen onto one of the ovens. The alarm was raised and the fire put out – there wasn't any thanks though, the Chairman said he'd rather have had the insurance money!'

As Notts moved from Division Four to the top flight, Brian resisted advances to move on but admits feeling disappointed that he did not get the opportunity to play in Division One. That disappointment was slightly tempered by the club granting Brian a testimonial to honour his loyalty and commitment to the club. The fans turned out in force to honour one of their greatest-ever stalwarts.

A lifelong resident of Keyworth, Brian briefly entered the non-League scene as a player before earning a living in 'structural repairs'. Always a keen fisherman his spare time is spent on the river banks, although his ex-side's fortunes are never far from his thoughts.

Brian Stubbs – a true giant in the history of Notts County.

Dean Thomas

Date of birth: 19 December 1961, Coventry

Notts County record:

Appearances: League 134, FA Cup 6, League Cup 11, Others 14
Goals: League 8, FA Cup 0, League Cup 0, Others 0
Debut: 24 March 1990 v Bristol City (h) drew 0–0

Also played for: Nuneaton Borough, Wimbledon, Alemania Aachen (Germany), Fortuna Dusseldorf (Germany), Northampton
    Town, Bedworth United
Managed: Bedworth United, Hinckley United

For sheer hard work and endeavour, few equalled Dean Thomas. He liked to get in where it hurts and get dirty. The tough-tackling midfielder played his part in both of County's Wembley play-off wins and pays tribute to his old boss. 'Obviously to play at Wembley is a dream for any footballer but Neil Warnock didn't want the players to be affected by the occasion, so the week before we were due to play Tranmere he took us all to watch the Leyland DAF Cup final there.'

The manager's attention to detail ensured there would be no surprises for the Notts lads – even the more experienced. 'I enjoyed it – it worked for me and helped with our preparation. I'd only ever been to Wembley once before – to watch Liverpool beat Bruges in the 1978 European Cup final.'

Dean is particularly grateful that he had the chance to go back the following year and sample a second play-off win beneath the Twin Towers. 'To be honest I probably celebrated a little too much after the first match and didn't take it all in – what it all meant really. The club doctor travelled on the coach with us for that game, just to sample the atmosphere. I think he thought it was like that every week!'

Notts elevation from the Third Division to the First, in successive seasons, meant that Dean was able to complete the set of playing at every level of the professional game. 'I'd played in the Fourth for Wimbledon.'

The chance for British players to move to the continent was still a novelty when Dean accepted an invitation, early in his career, to join Alemania Aachen in Germany. Family contacts helped set up the move. 'My brother Wayne was playing over there for Bayer Uerdingen – and had become the first English player to win a German cup winners' medal. He'd told me what to expect and I thoroughly enjoyed it at both Aachen and then when I moved to Dusseldorf.'

Dean returned to England to play for Northampton but was grateful when Notts came calling. 'I really wanted to make an impact on the game and Neil Warnock gave me that opportunity at Meadow Lane.' Throughout the next two years his consistency was a model to behold. His manager said of him, 'Dean was one of the most enthusiastic players I ever worked with and he packed the hardest left-foot shot I ever saw.' Despite that endorsement, Dean's goal output was modest: a 1990 winner against Portsmouth the player's pick of his eight Notts goals. 'We were awful that day and Mick Jones laid into me at half-time, saying I was the worst defensive midfielder he'd ever seen. I think the goal helped me back into his good books!'

When Mick Walker succeeded Neil Warnock he handed the captain's armband to Dean. 'That was a great honour – it really meant a lot. It was just a disappointment that I didn't wear it for very long, due to injury.' In a County Cup match against their cross-city rivals Dean was injured in a tackle with Forest's Carl Tiler. 'I'd even cancelled a weeks holiday to play in the game and knew it was a bad one straightaway.' Five operations and two frustrating years of rehabilitation brought an inevitable conclusion. 'The specialist told me to pack up playing at that level or risk not being able to walk again.'

Dean turned to coaching and for a short period actually took over as Notts boss. 'When they sacked Howard Kendall in 1995, they put Wayne Jones, Steve Nicol and myself in joint-charge. It only lasted for three months until Colin Murphy was brought in.' The new boss brought in his own staff and Dean moved on to Bedworth United as player-manager – 'the knee was OK to play at that level!' – before joining Hinckley United in time for the 1997–98 season.

Under Dean's management 'The Knitters' clinched the Dr Marten's Midland/Western championship in 2000–01. With former Notts star Charlie Palmer as first-team coach, Dean oversaw Hinckley's move to a brand new stadium in 2005, despite constant media speculation linking him with vacant Football League managerial vacancies.

Phil Turner

Date of birth: 12 February 1962, Sheffield

Notts County record:

Appearances: League 237, FA Cup 15, League Cup 20, Others 32

Goals: League 16, FA Cup 3, League Cup 0, Others 3

Debut: 4 March 1989 v Reading (a) won 3–1

Also played for: Lincoln City, Grimsby Town, Leicester City

It is usually the highlight of any footballer's career if he gets the opportunity to play at Wembley Stadium. Phil Turner was fortunate that, during his time with Notts County, he was able to achieve much, much more than that. As skipper, he led the side out at England's most famous sporting venue on four separate occasions. 'I remember reading that Bobby Moore once said he'd never get tired of coming out of that tunnel', says Phil. 'I have to keep reminding myself that I'm fortunate enough to know what he means. It's impossible to put into words how special it is.'

Phil arrived at Meadow Lane from Leicester City in an exchange deal which saw Gary Mills going the other way. He had had barely a year with the Foxes and had struggled to hold down a first-team place. After lengthy spells at Lincoln City, where he made 277 first-team appearances, and Grimsby Town, he was desperate for the opportunity of regular football.

'It's always a big decision when you change clubs because, no matter how much "homework" you do in advance, you are never quite sure how it will work out until you start playing matches. Going to Leicester wasn't a good decision on my part and I knew when I discovered that Notts County were interested that it was important to get it right this time.'

Although the move meant a drop in divisions, there was one important factor in the decision. 'One of the main reasons that I agreed in the end was because of Neil Warnock. I asked a number of people whose views I respected and they told me he was one of those people who just seems to attract success. That was good enough for me because I'd reached a stage in my career where I really wanted to be with a club which achieved something.'

After making his debut in a 3–1 away win at Reading – Paul Barnes scoring a hat-trick – Phil played in the final 16 games of the 1988–89 season. Nine of those matches were won but Notts finished five points short of the play-off positions. Nevertheless, the midfielder had already made an impression. Tenacious in the tackle and fiercely competitive, Phil's arrival brought some much-needed steel into the County 'engine room'.

His never-say-die attitude impressed his manager, who appointed Phil as club captain. Little did the player suspect at that stage but in consecutive seasons he would be climbing the steps to the Royal Box at Wembley in order to receive the trophy after Notts had won back-to-back play-off finals. Additionally, at the end of the 1989–90 season Phil won the supporters' Player of the Year award, an accolade he also received four years later.

Crucially, perhaps, injuries restricted Phil to just 29 appearances during the Magpies lone season in the top flight. Though of small comfort at the time, the relegation meant that Notts were eligible to compete in the Anglo-Italian Cup competition. Although there were many who criticised the addition of another low-key event in a crowded fixture list, it did enable County to make two more trips to the 'venue of legends'.

'For most of us it was the only chance we had of playing in any sort of European competition. We set out to enjoy ourselves and had the reward of reaching two finals. I thought we were unlucky against Brescia as I felt we were the better side and it made it even sweeter to go back and win the following year.'

At the end of the 1995–96 season, after more than 300 first-team games for Notts, Phil called time on his professional career. Between February and September 2004 he worked as assistant to former County teammate, Dave Norton, at Grantham Town and he pulled the black and white stripes on again during the summer of 2005 when he appeared for the Magpies in the Sky Sports' Masters tournament.

Mick Vinter

Date of birth: 23 May 1954, Boston, Lincolnshire

Notts County record:

Appearances: League 166, FA Cup 8, League Cup 10, Others 10

Goals: League 54, FA Cup 5, League Cup 1, Others 3

Debut: 12 August 1972 v Shrewsbury Town (a) drew 0–0

Also played for: Boston United, Wrexham, Oxford United, Mansfield Town, Newport County, Gainsborough Trinity, Kettering Town, Matlock Town, Oakham United, Hucknall Town, Sutton Town

Most decent strikers enjoy purple patches at some stage in their career. For Mick Vinter and Notts County, the spring of 1978 remains unforgettable. In six consecutive matches the Magpies registered just one goal in each game – all of them scored by Mick. The stretch was extended to a run of 8 goals in 9 matches – an incredible run of form by anyone's standards.

By the end of that 1977–78 season Mick Vinter had finished way ahead as the club's top scorer, totalling 19 in the League and another six in the cup competitions. His achievements were deservedly recognised with the supporters handing him the Player of the Year award.

Mick had been at Meadow Lane for almost six years by that stage of his career, having previously worn the colours of Boston United, his hometown club. Indeed, his roots made for an easy and obvious media nickname, 'The Lincolnshire Poacher'.

First-team opportunities were limited during his first couple of years at the Lane, although he did chip in with the odd goal whenever an opportunity arose to press his claims. Prolific in the reserves, Mick watched and waited as Les Bradd and Kevin Randall continued to justify their own selections up front. The 1976–77 season was probably the breakthrough season, with a healthy one-in-three goal ratio as the young striker scored 12 goals from 36 appearances in Division Two.

Amongst his haul was his first senior hat-trick, scored away at Millwall on 22 January 1977. Bradd added two more as County celebrated a famous 5–0 win in the capital. Away goals were becoming something of a speciality for Mick – of his 12, all but one were scored on the opposition's ground.

Under Jimmy Sirrel, County looked to be edging closer and closer to the top-flight promotion they would eventually gain. However, in the 1978–79 season they would go tantalisingly close before ending up with a sixth-placed finish. For the second year in a row Mick was again the club's leading scorer, this time with 14.

A 4–1 home win over Sheffield United brought another hat-trick but the failure to finish in the top two meant that Notts were prepared to listen to offers for their centre-forward. Wrexham's bid of £150,000 was more than County had ever received for any player and was too good an offer to turn down. 'Vint' went to North Wales and remained a prolific goalscorer around the lower leagues for many years. He returned to Nottinghamshire to help Mansfield Town to promotion from the Fourth Division in 1986.

Like many before him, he did the rounds of local non-League clubs, as well as combining a new career for himself as an insurance salesman.

Darren Ward

Date of birth: 11 May 1974, Worksop, Notts

Notts County record:

Appearances: League 252, FA Cup 22, League Cup 18, Others 10

Debut: 12 August 1995 v Wrexham (a) drew 1–1

Also played for: Mansfield Town, Nottingham Forest, Norwich City, Wales (5 caps)

Very few players have served all three of Nottinghamshire's Football League clubs with as much distinction as Darren Ward.

Born at Worksop, in the north of the county, Darren played in 81 League matches for Mansfield Town over a three-year period before joining up with the Magpies in the summer of 1995. The transfer fee was in the region of £150,000, which seemed good business from the outset, especially when he went on to become an ever-present during his first term at Meadow Lane.

Notts finished the campaign in fourth position and advanced to the play-off final at Wembley after their two-legged victory over Crewe Alexandra in the semi-final. The excitement of playing at the national stadium soon gave way to immense disappointment as Bradford City ended the Magpies' promotion aspirations with a two-goal victory.

At a height of 6ft 2in and weighing over 14 stone, Darren dominates the penalty area with his commanding presence. Coupled with his fine shot-stopping and decent dead-ball kicking, he appeared destined to rise to the very top of his profession. His progress was halted for a while when Notts went from one end of the League table to the other and were relegated to the bottom division at the end of the 1996–97 season.

The arrival of Sam Allardyce as County's boss certainly turned the club's fortunes around and the title was won in style at the first attempt to give Darren his first tangible reward in the game. Over the next three seasons he maintained a remarkable level of consistency and topped 250 League appearances for the club, emulating the likes of Steve Cherry, George Smith and the legendary Albert Iremonger in doing so.

After several squad call-ups Darren finally joined the rather exclusive list of Notts County players who have played international football, when he was selected to make his debut for Wales against Portugal in Chaves. The game unfortunately ended in a 3–0 defeat with the great Luis Figo scoring the first.

In May 2001, at the end of his contract, Darren moved across the river to join Nottingham Forest. During his three years with the City Ground club, the big goalie clocked up 123 League appearances and helped the Reds into the play-offs at the end of the 2002–03 season. He also gained further international recognition with four more caps for Wales.

In August 2004, 'Wardy' was on the move again, this time to join Norwich City, who were newly promoted to the Premiership. The spectacular form of Robert Green proved to be a stumbling block to Darren's first-team opportunities, restricting him to just one substitute appearance throughout the whole season.

With time still very much on his side, there's every chance that Darren Ward may one day return to play in Nottinghamshire again – and all Magpies fans will be hoping that if it does happen then it will be for County!

Neil Warnock

Date of birth: 1 December 1948, Sheffield

Notts County record:

Manager: January 1989–January 1993

Played for: Chesterfield, Rotherham United, Hartlepool United, Scunthorpe United, Aldershot, Barnsley, York City

Also managed: Gainsborough Trinity, Burton Albion, Scarborough, Huddersfield Town, Plymouth Argyle, Oldham Athletic, Bury, Sheffield United

Neil Warnock's achievements at Meadow Lane should never be underestimated. In taking Notts from the old Third Division to the top flight in successive seasons he fulfilled, what many saw, as an impossible dream.

Wherever their affiliations lie, there will not be a football supporter in the land who does not have an opinion of Neil. While it is true that much of the aura around him has been cultivated by the man himself, he is often unfairly portrayed as being a tough, argumentative so-and-so who will pull any stunt to give his side an edge. Those that lean towards that conception overlook his record of achievements and the feelings of those that have played under him. Neil will always back his players to the hilt and praise them regardless, providing they are giving of their best. What he will not stand for are those that short-change him.

In his own words, he was an average player, who did the rounds at a succession of lower League clubs. 'I was a right-winger but could play up front. To describe me as a journeyman pro would be kind really - I was pretty quick but brainless!' During his time at Hartlepool, Neil served under a man who was to become one of the biggest influences on his career. 'Len Ashurst was manager and a lot of what he taught me I still incorporate today. His pre-season routines were excellent and he really knew how to bring the best out of a player.'

Neil cut his managerial teeth at Gainsborough and Burton before leading Scarborough to the Conference title and a place in the Football League. On 5 January 1989 he was appointed manager of Notts County but kicked off his reign with a 0–2 defeat at Swansea.

A ninth-placed finish was as good as Notts could have hoped for after a disappointing start to the season, but the next two years brought untold joy to supporters who had always hoped to see their favourites play at Wembley. In consecutive years Neil's side reached the end-of-season play-off final and triumphed on both occasions. While the players deserve considerable credit, the manager was undeniably the catalyst.

As a man-manager and motivator, Neil has had few equals. His training methods were revolutionary and have brought suitable rewards. Days at the seaside, at theme parks or out in the countryside were just as likely to be on the training programme as cross-country runs or sessions with the weights. The players responded and gave Neil the utmost respect. Chelsea, famously, tried to woo him to Stamford Bridge but he chose to show loyalty and remain at Meadow Lane.

Sadly, the good times dried up and Notts' stay in the top flight lasted for only one season. Once on the downward spiral, it became hard to halt the slide and a poor start to the 1992–93 campaign brought about calls for a change – Neil's tenure was over.

He was not out of the game for long and, predictably, success continued to come his way. A move to Huddersfield Town brought about a fourth promotion in nine years and then another was achieved when he joined Plymouth Argyle. After short stints at Oldham and Bury he joined the club he had supported as a youngster, Sheffield United, whom he led to semi-final appearances in both the domestic cup competitions and another play-off final.

Although the Blades have not yet found the glory they yearn for, they know they have a man in charge who cares every bit as much as the fan on the terrace. Everywhere that Neil Warnock has been, he has instilled a sense of togetherness and unity in his squad.

Whatever his final list of achievements, Neil will always be able to look back on a job well done while he was at Meadow Lane. In turn, the County fans will never forget him.

Dave Watson

Date of birth: 5 October 1946, Stapleford, Notts

Notts County record:
Appearances: League 50, FA Cup 1, League Cup 2
Goals: League 2, FA Cup 0, League Cup 0
Debut: 28 March 1967 v Chester (h) won 3–0

Also played for: Rotherham United, Sunderland, Manchester City, Werder Bremen (Germany), Southampton, Stoke City, Derby County, Kettering Town, England (65 caps)

Better known as one of England's finest ever centre-halves, Dave Watson was actually employed as a striker during his early days at Notts County. 'I could run around a bit then and they thought I was going to be one of those "utility" players – able to play in a number of positions.'

Dave made just four appearances in his first season with Notts. 'I remember playing at Tranmere on the last day. We lost 3–0 but all the goals were from long-range shots. Every time they tried their luck, the ball found its target.'

Despite being a first-team novice at the time, Dave remembers that it was a fairly bleak time for the club. 'We were fighting against re-election and playing in front of just two or three thousand every week. Although I was only 20 I knew how important it was that we managed to stay in the League and try and turn the club's fortunes around.'

The glamorous world of professional football certainly left a lot to be desired, for the young Watson. 'Our wages weren't great, at the best of times, but in the summer we had to make do without any bonuses of any sort. To supplement my income I worked on the fruit stalls on Nottingham market. A lot of the players did something similar. The owners were fans and liked to do their bit for us.'

In the first half of the 1967–68 season Dave enjoyed a lengthy run in the County side, although he was frequently switched about between defence and attack. His first goal for the club came at home against Crewe Alexandra, enough to secure a 1–0 win.

Unbeknown to Dave, enquiries were being made about his availability. In early 1968 the club accepted a bid from Rotherham United. 'I didn't even know where Rotherham was', he admitted later. After a couple of seasons at Millmoor, with summers still being spent on Nottingham market, came a move which was to ignite the career of Dave Watson.

Sunderland boss Alan Brown paid £100,000 to take him to Roker Park. By now, fully converted to a strapping, central defender, Dave went on to enjoy a highly successful period on Wearside, culminating in the shock FA Cup final victory over Leeds United in 1973.

A year later he won his first England cap against Portugal. It was to be Sir Alf Ramsey's final game in charge of the national side. For Dave, it signified the start of an eight-year stint as an international regular – an era when he had few equals in his position. Dave skippered England on three occasions, against Romania, Wales and Scotland in 1981, but would dearly have loved to have done it more often. 'I hoped I'd get the armband for my 50th cap against Argentina at Wembley in 1980. They were the World Champions and had a young Maradona in their side – and we played them off the park with a 3–1 win.'

After leaving Sunderland, Dave played for a succession of other sides before returning to his hometown club. 'I'd retired really but Larry Lloyd invited me to come back to Notts to assist him. After a couple of months Larry got the sack and Richie Barker took over. He'd been my boss at Stoke City and we got on well and he persuaded me to carry on playing for another season, which I thoroughly enjoyed.'

Dave settled in the Nottingham area, where he runs his own promotions business and just occasionally gets the chance to see the Magpies in action. 'I'll always be fond of the club – it's where I began and ended my career. Although I wasn't there for long on either occasion, the supporters were always good to me and I've never forgotten that.'

Jack Wheeler

Date of birth: 13 July 1919, Evesham, Worcestershire

Notts County record:

Trainer/Coach/Physio: 1957–83, including 14-month period as caretaker manager from September 1968 to November 1969

Played for: Cheltenham Town, Birmingham City, Huddersfield Town, Kettering Town

Despite never having played for the club Jack Wheeler's influence upon Notts County can never be overestimated. As trainer, coach and caretaker manager, Jack did not miss a single match for 26 years. Quite rightly, his achievements have been recognised, with the club awarding Jack a Life Membership and a permanent seat in the Meadow Lane directors' box.

Jack's playing days were spent as a goalkeeper, beginning his career in the Southern League with Cheltenham Town. On 16 March 1938 he was transferred to Birmingham City, as understudy to England's Harry Hibbs. 'Harry couldn't have been more helpful towards me. I always vowed that if I ever reached the stage in my career where people wanted my advice, then I would try and be as helpful as he had been towards me.'

Jack made six Division One appearances for the St Andrews side before being called up to serve his country during the war. 'I joined the Sixth Armoured Division and served in North Africa and Italy. When I returned home I made the odd 'guest appearance' for Birmingham at 30 shillings a game but Gilbert Merrick had joined the club, so I moved to Huddersfield when League football resumed.'

During the 1952–53 season Jack was part of a unique back unit. 'Our entire back six, myself, the two full backs and the three wing halves, all played in every one of the 42 League games. For a while it was recorded in the *Guinness Book of Records* – it'll certainly never be done again!'

Jack moved on to Kettering Town as player-coach under Tommy Lawton and followed the former County player to Meadow Lane. 'I'd been helping out with coaching at Kettering and they wanted me to stay and become manager but I considered it a great honour when Tommy asked me to move with him.'

So, in 1957, Jack's long association with the Magpies began. 'I was coach but had always been fascinated with the treatment of injuries. I'd had three fractures during my own playing career and had taken an active interest in my own recovery each time. This developed into something I enjoyed doing and eventually I gained the training and experience to do it properly.'

A succession of managers came and went at Notts before Jack was given the reins in a caretaker capacity. 'The chairman, Mr Dunnett, asked me to take over for a while. I ended up doing it for 14 months and for £30 a week, plus petrol expenses, I was manager, coach, physio and scout – not bad value for the club!'

To his own immense delight Jack was relieved of some of the burden when Jimmy Sirrel was appointed manager in November 1969. 'A lovely man and an honest man. You never got anything second hand from Jimmy – he would always tell you what he thought. He was a first-class coach who believed that footballers were better served by playing football every day on the training ground and not by running around a track.' Sirrell's Scottish accent was a constant source of amusement to his players, as was the pet name of 'Jackson', which he would call his able assistant.

County's elevation from the Fourth Division to the top flight was witnessed in its entirety by Jack, who clocked up his 1000th game with the club during the 1979–80 season. Fittingly his proudest moment was just around the corner. 'To be at Stamford Bridge when we beat Chelsea to reach Division One was the undoubted highlight. To think we would be lining up against the likes of Liverpool and Arsenal was just amazing.'

Jack eventually retired in 1983, having been involved in a total of 1,398 first-team games for the Magpies. He has continued to follow the fortunes of County ever since, including their glory days at Wembley. 'The play-off finals and the Anglo-Italian matches were great days for the club and I was proud to be there to witness them.'

Jack lives in Wollaton, in the same accommodation he was given when he first joined Notts. 'It used to be a club house – but they kindly sold it to me many years ago', he adds.

Over the years, hundreds of Notts County players have had the privilege of working with Jack Wheeler and they would all testify that he was one of the nicest, most helpful men in the game. Harry Hibbs would have been proud!

Devon White

Date of birth: 2 March 1964, Nottingham

Notts County record:

Appearances: League 55, FA Cup 4, League Cup 7, Others 6

Goals: League 19, FA Cup 1, League Cup 7, Others 2

Debut: 26 December 1994 v Millwall (h) lost 0–1

Also played for: Arnold Town, Lincoln City, Boston United, Bristol Rovers, Cambridge United, Queens Park Rangers, Watford, Shrewsbury Town, Ilkeston Town

Most footballers would give their eyeteeth to play at Wembley Stadium. Devon White not only achieved that distinction twice, he managed to score on both occasions – one of them a winning goal for Notts County.

The Anglo-Italian Cup competition had plenty of detractors down the years but few Magpies supporters would look upon it with anything other than affection. County reached the final in successive years, losing to Brescia in 1994 but triumphing the following year against Ascoli.

With the scores level at 1-1, Devon experienced his moment of glory. 'The ball was played out right and a perfect cross came in. I managed to get a really good connection on the ball and powered a header downwards. The ball took a bounce and went over the diving 'keeper.' Although it was a bitterly cold spring afternoon, and only 11,000 were present, Notts County had won a knock-out competition at the home of football – reason enough for the players to celebrate. 'For many of us, it was the highlight of our careers', says Devon. 'Certainly we felt a great sense of pride as we went up to get our medals and lift the cup.'

The big striker could enjoy the celebrations as much as anyone because he knew what it meant to the travelling fans. 'I was born in Nottingham and brought up on Brand Street, around half a mile from the ground. As a youngster one of my first memories was of hearing the roar of the crowd on a Saturday afternoon.' Despite his close proximity to Meadow Lane it was another club that Devon favoured at the time. 'Trevor Brooking was always my favourite player, so I followed West Ham as a youngster.'

The young goalscorer gained a reputation with Arnold Town before being given his break, in the professional ranks, by Colin Murphy at Lincoln City. After two years at Sincil Bank and then a season with Boston United, Devon headed to the South West where he enjoyed a long and fruitful spell with Bristol Rovers. 'We really did have a great time at Rovers. While I was there we won the League and I'd played and scored in a Leyland DAF final at Wembley.' After making over 200 League appearances for the 'Pirates', Devon played in brief spells at both QPR and Cambridge United but was soon on his way back 'home'. 'Colin Murphy had known me from my time at Lincoln and signed me for Notts', says Devon.

Despite his goal against Ascoli, 'Big Dev' recalls another cup occasion during his time with the Magpies. 'We played Leeds United at home in the League Cup, having drawn the first leg. We lost 3–2 and I scored our first goal but I'll always remember it because it was the first time in my career I was asked to take a penalty. Fortunately, I managed to stick it past John Lukic in the Leeds goal.'

Nowadays Devon works as an electrician and seldom puts the boots on, although he did play in the Legends match at Meadow Lane. 'I really enjoyed turning out again and it was for such a good cause. I'm really pleased that things did turn out well for County in the end because they've always been such a friendly club, with a great tradition.'

Howard Wilkinson

Date of birth: 13 November 1943, Sheffield

Notts County record:
Manager: August 1982–June 1983

Played for: Sheffield Wednesday, Brighton and Hove Albion, Boston United
Also managed: Boston United, Mossley, England Under-21s, Sheffield Wednesday, Leeds United, Sunderland, England (caretaker manager for two matches)

When Howard Wilkinson returned to Notts County in December 2004 as a non-executive director, he gave the most heartening reason imaginable to supporters. 'Because I care', he said.

Working with Jimmy Sirrel some 20 years earlier, Howard had helped achieve the impossible dream of overseeing Notts County's promotion to the old First Division. Tactically astute, his attention to detail complemented the manager's less orthodox methods and ensured that nothing would be left to chance. The young coach had been involved with the England Under-21s and his fresh approach ensured that the players clearly enjoyed some innovative training sessions. 'I was very fortunate', says Howard, 'to have worked with people like Ron Greenwood, Bobby Robson, Don Howe, Terry Venables and Dave Sexton. You can't help but learn a little bit from coaches of that quality.'

Howard had enjoyed moderate success playing on the wing for Sheffield Wednesday and Brighton before entering the non-League scene with Boston United. When Jim Smith left York Street in 1972, Howard initially took over as player-coach before leading the Pilgrims to two consecutive Northern Premier League titles. Via Mossley and the England set-up he arrived at Meadow Lane in December 1979.

Howard soon discovered that there were a few characters on County's books. 'I'd only been at the club a short while when we took the players to a hotel for New Year's Eve. We were due to play Cambridge United the next day and we felt the players needed to prepare properly. We all had a meal and went to bed but at around 12.15am I could hear plenty of noise and rang reception. They told me it was coming from one of our rooms. I went along the corridor and knocked on the door, to be greeted by Iain McCulloch, who was holding a can. Behind him, in a room full of smoke, were 11 of the 13 players who'd supposedly gone to bed!'

The promotion season of 1980–81 will never be forgotten and the coach was confident of success from the start. 'When I'd joined the club Jimmy had told me that the players "could nae feckin' run!" I discovered that he was right so we worked hard on devising a way of playing where they didn't have to run. Pre-season was hard, five days a week, mornings and afternoons. Everything was rehearsed over and over again, like a formation dancing team.'

Confidence was high within the squad. 'The players knew we were looking sharp – the bookies still had us at something like 66/1 to go up and Don Masson went round everybody asking for a tenner!' The historic afternoon at Chelsea remains Howard's favourite County memory, although he is proud to have succeeded Jimmy and managed the club for one season in the top flight.

Howard was attracted by the opportunity to return to his old club Sheffield Wednesday and he managed them to promotion, before taking over at Leeds United, with whom he enjoyed great success. The Elland Road club earned Howard yet another promotion, in the 1989–90 season, and just two years later they won the First Division championship. This was the season before the Premiership was introduced and Howard remains the last Englishman to win the top domestic honour.

An appointment as the FA's Technical Director followed, during which he was twice asked to take over as the caretaker boss of the full national side. In February 1999 he was in charge for a home friendly against France after Glenn Hoddle had stepped down and the opportunity arose again in October 2000 for a World Cup qualifier in Finland, shortly after Kevin Keegan's resignation.

A return to club football followed, with a year at Sunderland before he rejoined Notts in December 2004, as a non-executive director. 'Notts County gave me my start in the Football League. But my position does not preclude me getting on the training ground and doing all the things I have been doing for the past few years. I also care about the future of this club and clubs like it who are an important part of the bigger picture.'

Aside from his duties with the Magpies, Howard presides as the Chairman of the League Managers' Association.

Kelvin Wilson

Date of birth: 3 September 1985, Nottingham

Notts County record (to end of season 2004–05):
Appearances: League 44, FA Cup 4, League Cup 2, Others 1
Goals: League 2, FA Cup 0, League Cup 1, Others 0
Debut: 17 April 2004 v Hartlepool United (a) lost 0–4

It is often difficult to assess how far a talented youngster can go in the professional game but many shrewd judges believe that Notts County have found themselves a defender with immense potential in Kelvin Wilson.

Associated with his home-town club since his days in the Under-13 side, Kelvin has watched Notts for as long as he can remember. 'I used to enjoy watching Devon White and Gary Owers play and when I started playing in the youth teams we would be given free passes to get in and watch the matches.'

Kelvin graduated through Notts' youth ranks and was soon making a big impression as a rapidly-developing central defender. Possessing the necessary attributes to succeed – pace, strength and determination – it was only a question of when he would be thrust into the first-team spotlight. His debut, away at Hartlepool, could have arrived in happier circumstances. Notts were already trailing 3–0 when he was thrust on as a 67th minute substitute for David Pipe. Soon it was 4–0 and game over – 'I was as disappointed as the rest of the team at the result but inside I was very proud to have played for the first team.'

The 2003–04 season ended with Kelvin clocking up his first two starts for the club, sending him into the summer break with high hopes for the new season. 'I was pleased with the way things were progressing but knew I'd got an awful lot to learn if I was to remain in contention for a first-team place. Everyone was telling me to remain level-headed but I knew that I'd only just started on the learning curve.'

'Kelv' did far more than remain in contention – he cemented a place in the side and featured in 41 League games during the 2004–05 campaign. The quality of his performances was noted by those around him – as well as the fans – and the campaign ended with Kelvin scooping the club's Players' Player of the Year award, the most Improved Player award and the Nottinghamshire Footballer of the Year award.

'I really enjoyed getting a regular run in the side', he says. 'There were lots of people giving me plenty of good advice but, in particular, I have Ian Richardson, Mike Whitlow and John Gaunt to thank. They were all massive influences on my development. Obviously Ian and Mike are vastly experienced defenders themselves and John was always available if I wanted to talk about how things had gone.' Switching between the right-back berth and a position in the centre of defence, Kelvin came on in leaps and bounds during a season which saw Notts floundering at the wrong end of the table. Despite a sequence of poor results, the young defender began to make his own headlines, for all the right reasons. Some of the nation's bigger clubs were rumoured to be interested in Kelvin. 'People began to say that I was being watched by so and so but I know I've got to keep grafting and learning my trade. I love being a Notts County player and am very happy at the club.'

Kelvin had some first-hand experience of coping with Premiership forwards when he faced Middlesbrough in an FA Cup-tie at Meadow Lane in January 2005. 'We got the dream start, going ahead early on, and everyone was really buzzing at half-time. They showed their class in the second half though – it was good experience to play against them, even though we eventually lost 2–1.'

Always happy to venture forward for set-plays, Kelvin garnished his first full season by registering three goals – his first for the club. His debut strike came in a League Cup match away against West Ham United. 'It was quite an occasion to get my first goal', says Kelvin. 'Rob Ullathorne hit a long free-kick into the box, Ian Richardson helped it on, Glynn Hurst chipped it back and I was able to head it in from just a couple of yards out. Although we lost I'll always enjoy the memory and thought that I had a decent game overall.'

A couple more goals followed, in the League matches away at Darlington and Wycombe. 'I really wanted to get a goal at Meadow Lane before the end of the season', he admits. 'Hopefully there'll be plenty more opportunities for me to do so in the future.' While wishing Kelvin every success in his career, Magpies supporters will echo those sentiments and hope he remains an integral member of their defence for many more years to come.

Kevin Wilson

Date of birth: 18 April 1961, Banbury

Notts County record:

Appearances:	League 69, FA Cup 2, League Cup 4, Others 6
Goals:	League 3, FA Cup 0, League Cup 0, Others 0
Debut:	28 March 1992 v Crystal Palace (h) lost 2–3

Also played for: Banbury United, Derby County, Ipswich Town, Chelsea, Bradford City, Walsall, Northampton Town, Northern Ireland (42 caps)

Managed: Northampton Town, Bedford Town, Aylesbury United, Kettering Town

Up front, midfield, sweeper, full-back – it did not really matter to Kevin Wilson, he was just happy to play. In a full and varied career, which spanned 22 years, Kevin played over 700 matches and scored more than 200 goals. 'It was a nice milestone to reach – 200', he reflects. 'I would also liked to have reached 50 caps but that wasn't to be – but I'm satisfied with how my career turned out.' As it was Kevin represented Northern Ireland on 42 occasions, qualifying through his mother's place of birth. The 16 caps he won during his time at Meadow Lane make him the club's most-capped player of all time.

Kevin joined Notts towards the end of the 1991–92 season, with relegation from the top flight only a matter of weeks away. His debut typified the club's fortunes at the time. 'I lifted the ball over Nigel Martyn to put us 2–0 up against Crystal Palace but they still came back and beat us 3–2.' That result was perhaps an indication of how things would turn out at Meadow Lane. 'Maybe it wasn't the right club at the right time for me. I was offered a new contract at Chelsea but felt I was some way down the pecking order. I just wanted to play and Neil Warnock offered me that chance at County.'

Having played as a striker throughout most of his time at Derby County and Chelsea, Kevin was continually switched around by Neil Warnock and then Mick Walker. "In goal was the only place they didn't put me. From a professional point of view it was a little bit infuriating but they knew I could do a job for the side in most positions.'

A wealth of experience, gained playing in the top flight and internationals, enabled Kevin to become something of a father figure to several of the Notts youngsters. 'We had a good crop of young players coming through at that time, people like Richard Walker, Paul Cox, Steve Slawson and Michael Simpson. I saw it as part of my role to help with their development as much as I could.'

Kevin is amongst the select few to have played at Wembley for the Magpies, albeit in a losing cause. 'I played in the Anglo-Italian Cup final defeat to Brescia. We were desperately disappointed to lose because we felt we should have won the match but I did manage to get my own little bit of revenge on one of their players. Gheorghe Hagi had played for the Italian side on the Sunday and then I lined up against him when his Romanian national side came to Belfast on the following Wednesday. Hagi was sent off and we beat them 2–0.'

Playing mainly as a full-back during his final season at the Lane, Kevin accepted an offer to move to Walsall as player-coach. The opportunity was too good to resist. 'I felt that I was being written off in some quarters and wanted a fresh challenge – I wanted to prove myself again. The fans had been brilliant towards me but overall I was disappointed with the way it had gone at Notts.' The Saddlers benefited from Kevin's return to a striking role. 'I scored something like 49 goals in 137 appearances for Walsall, so I'm pleased I made the move.'

Management was always going to be a natural progression for the forward-thinking Wilson. His philosophy on the job is interesting. 'I liken it to a moving train. As a player you are just one of the trucks being pulled along with the rest – as the manager you are the train driver doing the steering.' Train driver Kevin won promotion while in charge at Northampton Town but then moved into the non-League game. Since Boxing Day 2003 he has been at the helm in charge of Nationwide North side, Kettering Town.

Bob Worthington

Date of birth: 22 April 1947, Halifax

Notts County record:

Appearances: League 232, FA Cup 14, League Cup 10
Goals: League 1, FA Cup 0, League Cup 0
Debut: 14 September 1968 v Darlington (a) lost 2–3

Also played for: Middlesbrough, Southend United

One of Billy Gray's last acts as manager of Notts County was to complete the double signing of Don Masson and Bob Worthington from Middlesbrough. While Masson was soon elevated to the international fold, County fans will recall that it was a decent bit of business to acquire Bob as well. 'They got us both for about £7,000', says the Yorkshireman, and adds, 'I think I was the £500 bit!'

'I'd actually gone and had a look round at Meadow Lane the year before when there was a possibility that I'd be moving. So when it happened, I knew what to expect but I'd only been there a couple of weeks when Billy was sacked.'

Notts were languishing at the lower end of the Football League and began their recovery with Jack Wheeler in temporary charge. 'He actually did a very good job and tightened us up at the back. Although we drew plenty, we suddenly became much harder to beat.'

The baton was then handed to Jimmy Sirrel, an eye-opening experience for the players. 'When we first met him we were all looking at each other. We really didn't know what to make of him and we couldn't understand him.' That first impression did not last long, as Bob reflects. 'Jimmy really was a character but he was very good at his job. He was so thorough, everything was rehearsed over and over again on the training field. He had his own style and really was a one-off but he instilled a great team spirit within us. For some reason though, he's always called me "Robert eh".'

Bob was an ever-present in the Division Four championship side, a left-back who took no prisoners and rarely mistimed a challenge. In more than 250 first-team matches for Notts, Bob only managed to get himself on the scoresheet on one occasion, at home to Rotherham United in March 1972. 'It was a miserable, cold evening and we were trailing 1–0 with about 10 minutes to go. I made a run forward in the centre of the park. Don Masson saw me and squared the ball perfectly for me to hit, left-footed, from about 20 yards. It flew in – it might have been my only goal but it was worth waiting for!'

David Greenwood from Thrumpton has supported Notts for almost 40 years and recalls the rather unusual goal celebration. 'Bob possessed an awesome left foot but occasionally was on the receiving end of some unkind banter from the crowd. When he scored his goal he exacted revenge by running in front of the County Road Stand and dropping his shorts to the crowd!'

Bob explains what happened. 'The supporters were really moaning that night. We knew we weren't playing well but they were making it worse. I just did it on the spur of the moment but thought I'd get it in the neck from the manager. After the match he walked into the dressing room and looked at me. Everyone went quiet until he said, "Well done Robert eh, you did right!" '

The following season Notts gained promotion again, finishing as runners-up to Bolton Wanderers and Bob recalls that it was a match against the Lancashire side that turned the club's fortunes. 'We really weren't doing very well in the first half of the season, losing far too many matches. In the period between Christmas and New Year we went to Bolton and trailed 2–0 at half-time. Jimmy was almost in tears at the break – he couldn't believe we were struggling so badly. He looked almost pathetic as he pleaded with us, "Come on lads you can still do it." I don't know why but we were brilliant in the second half and got a 2–2 draw. We never looked back after then. That one half of football gave us all our confidence back again.'

Having hardly missed a game in five years at Meadow Lane, Bob's position came under threat towards the end of the 1973–74 season and he decided to move on. 'I told Jimmy I wouldn't be back for pre-season as I needed first-team football. Basic wages weren't very good if you weren't in the side so I needed to be playing somewhere. When I didn't come back he knew I meant it and helped me get sorted by setting up my move to Southend United.'

Bob spent just a year at Roots Hall before retiring from the game to run a small chain of sports shops. He moved to France for a couple of years before returning to the Halifax area but still keeps in touch with many of his old teammates.

With brothers Frank and Dave also having played professional football there was certainly plenty of talent in the Worthington family – but, as David Greenwood emphasises, 'Bob will always be remembered as a true County legend.'

Ron Wylie

Date of birth: 6 August 1933, Glasgow

Notts County record:

Appearances: League 227, FA Cup 10

Goals: League 35, FA Cup 3

Debut: 13 October 1951 v Doncaster Rovers (h) won 1–0

Also played for: Clydesdale, Aston Villa, Birmingham City

Managed: West Bromwich Albion

Although he later went on to serve several other clubs with distinction, Ron Wylie began a lifetime's involvement in League football at Notts County.

In truth, his footballing days began with Scottish junior side Clydesdale but he was in the Magpies first team shortly after his 18th birthday and was soon making a big impression. The young inside-forward did not score in any of the five matches he played in during autumn 1951, although his performances suggested that he had the potential to make it in the professional game. He had to wait until the penultimate match of the season before getting another opportunity – and how he took it!

Tommy Lawton had left Notts County in March 1952 and the fans were desperate to hail a new star. Ron put himself in the frame with a virtuoso performance on 19 April. Playing against a strong Birmingham City side, who were pressing for promotion, Ron grabbed four goals in a scintillating 5–0 victory – his first senior goals for the Magpies.

Rather than develop into an out-and-out goalscorer Ron became the linchpin between midfield and attack. A strong runner and decent tackler, he was comfortable in possession and his all-round vision helped create opportunities for those around him.

During the remaining years of the 1950s Ron was one of the first names on the team sheet. He was an ever-present throughout the 1954–55 season, when he registered a dozen goals – 10 of them in the League. That was his best return, although he did record another hat-trick for Notts – at home to Bristol Rovers in December 1955.

Injuries blighted Ron's last couple of years with County. By then the team had slid into Division Three and were struggling at the wrong end of the table. Frank Hill was brought in as manager and told he could only generate funds by selling players.

Aston Villa were alerted and stepped in with a bid of £9,500 for Ron, which the club were forced to accept. His final match was a 1–1 draw against Stockport County, with Tony Hateley getting the Notts goal on his debut.

Ron's move to Villa Park was a great success and he was able to collect a League Cup winners' medal in 1961. He stayed there for seven seasons before crossing the second city to join fierce rivals, Birmingham City.

When Ron eventually hung up his boots he had compiled a career total of 551 League appearances but, desperate to stay in the game, he turned to coaching. He gained valuable experience in Cyprus and Hong Kong before returning to the West Midlands. He served on the backroom staff at Coventry City, Aston Villa and West Brom before succeeding Ronnie Allen as Albion's first-team manager, from 1982 to 1984.

Later he returned to Villa Park, extending his service there to over 25 years, the latter part of which he served as the club's Community Liaison Officer.

Dean Yates

Place of birth: 26 October 1967, Leicester

Notts County record:

Appearances: League 314, FA Cup 20, League Cup 24, Others 36
Goals: League 33, FA Cup 0, League Cup 0, Others 4
Debut: 6 April 1985 v Wimbledon (h) lost 2–3

Also played for: Derby County, Watford

The esteem in which Dean Yates is regarded was emphasised to the full during 2005 when the Ex-Notts County Players' Association held a dinner in his honour and awarded him a 'Lifetime Achievement Award'. 'It was a wonderful gesture', says the former central defender. 'I've made many wonderful friends during my time with Notts and this accolade made me very proud indeed.' Although his final years with the club were cruelly interrupted by injury, Dean played almost 400 first-team games for the Magpies, giving nothing less than total commitment throughout.

Dean started his career training with his home-town's youth team until receiving a fairly damning assessment of his capabilities. 'They sent me a letter saying I needed to improve my heading, passing and tackling – there isn't much else is there?'

Undaunted, Dean continued to play Sunday morning football until being spotted by Garth Butler, a Notts scout, who invited him to Meadow Lane for trials. Things happened fairly rapidly from then on. 'I started my apprenticeship but within a year I was in the first team.' He still remembers his first goal. 'It was the winner at home to Bolton – a header at the far post.'

In only his second full season, Dean won the Player of the Year award but was disappointed to miss the final four games of the season. 'I wanted to play in every match as we were pushing for the play-offs but I broke my wrist, sliding into Carlisle's goalkeeper.' The following season Dean did maintain an ever-present record but, despite him scoring against Walsall in both legs of the play-off semi-finals, Notts again fell short.

Commanding in the air and tactically astute, the big defender did at last gain some tangible reward when Notts won their two play-off finals under Neil Warnock. 'The first time we went to Wembley was very special. It wasn't just a County thing – it was a big day for the whole city and I know a lot of Forest fans went and supported us.'

Dean remembers that there was a general calmness about the day itself. 'I don't think we had any "big-time Charlies" in the side and that helped. We all got on and we were all very relaxed and didn't really feel the pressure. On the morning of the game we just went to Wembley and had a casual stroll around the stadium.' A year later and Notts were back for another big clash in the capital. 'I think there was a bit more pressure on us against Brighton. Nobody really fancied us to win, so afterwards we were all a bit in shock. Then the reality hit home that we would be playing the likes of Arsenal and Manchester United.'

The fixture computer sent the Magpies to Old Trafford on the opening day but the first home match seemed a little more appetising. 'I'd always said I didn't want to leave Notts until I'd helped get them into the top flight so I was thrilled to get the goal which clinched our first win, against Southampton. Dean Thomas crossed a free-kick to the far post and I got up above Neil Ruddock to head it in.'

On 26 October 1991, Notts went to Highbury to face Arsenal. 'I don't know when it happened but my knee took a knock in that game. I tried to continue but had to come off. They thought it was a cartilage but it turned out to be much more serious than that. There was cruciate ligament damage as well and in the end I had to have the knee totally reconstructed.'

In all, Dean was out of the game for two years – though he should have returned much earlier. 'I'd had screws put in and should have been ready to have them out when one broke loose and I had to have another operation and it all reset again.'

Soon after returning to the game Derby County put in a bid for his services and a deal was arranged. 'The time was probably right to move on. I'd been out for two years and I felt I was being labelled as a bit injury-prone. All the problems though had been with the knee.' After more than three years at Derby and a couple of seasons at Watford, the knee flared up again. 'I had to have three or four more operations, making a total of 10 in all since that day at Arsenal.'

Dean began scouting for Derby County, while he assessed his future. 'I would have liked to have coached but the knee just wouldn't have allowed it.' Then came an offer he could not refuse – working alongside Colin Slater as the match summariser on BBC Radio Nottingham for all Notts County's matches. 'Colin makes it very easy for me but it's nice to still be involved and watching County every week. At times it's not been great but the fans have been remarkably loyal and I'm sure the good times will be along again soon.'

Roll of Honour

Matthew Abbott

Michael Adcock

Jim Atkins

Lee Atkins

Tony Baker

John Frank Baker

Martyn Bartram

Oliver Beeby

Mark Betts

James Bingham

Richard Bingham

Ian Birley

Peter Birley

Richard Blaney

Simon Peter Bradley

Matthew Gordon Bradley

Ian Brewster

Graeme Bunting

Raymond Burrows

Gerry Carver

Justin Cast

David Chapman

Dr Mick Chappell

Bryce John Clare

Carolanne Clark

Nick Clark

Hazel Clark

Sue Codrington

Alan Cooke

James Cooke

Ian Cooksey

A.R. Cooper

Barrie Cousins

Jackie Davenport

Matthew Dawson

Ian Devonport

Les Dowding

Richard Dowen-Jones

Brian Downes

Raymond Dowse

Steve Dring

Adey Dring

Mark Durkin

David Fells

Adam Paul Firman

Neil Fletcher

Malcolm Fletcher

Chris Furniss

Ian Gill	Clive Linley
Uwe Gould	Tony Mack
Julian Goulsbra	Mark Maltby
Jeff Grain	Michael Manning
David Greenwood	Steven Middleton
Philip Hall	Alan Middleton
Joanne Harley	Ian J. Mills
Michael Harrison	Michael Morgan
Scott Harrison	Peter Morris
Craig Hatfield	Clive Newman
G. Hayes	Stephen Newton
Michael Hennigan	Robert Ogg
Mark Hoskins	Antony Oliver
Thomas Hubery	Jim Orme
Richard Hucknall	Colin W. Parker
Ian Hudson	Tim Parker
Ron Hudson	David K. Parker
Richard (Rocky) Hudson	Michael R. Patterson
Helen Moffat	Robbie Patterson
Terry Jayes	Jim Perkins
Toby Jennison	Matthew Pickard
Michael Kaye	John B. Pritchard
Ivor Kirkham	Neil A. Pritchard
John E. Lamb	Darren Pryer
Alison Lamb	Andrew Rayson
Ian Langham	Bruce Rhodes

Mike Richardson
Jack William Richardson
David Richmond
Philip Rippon
Robert Robotham
Paul Rowbotham
Kenneth M. Rowe
Leslie Rowley
John Rudge
Matthew Sharman
Joy Sharpe
Richard Sheldon
Steve Shephard
Yvonne Shephard
Steve Shepherd
Ben Shepherd
Ralph Shepherd
Jack Shepherd
Alex Shepherd
Tony Slater
Ian Sloan
John Smalley
S.A. Smedley
Geoff Smeeton

Barry Smith
Trevor R. Smith
Warren H. Smith
Malc Smith
Charles Smith
Barrie Smith
Philip Smith
Jeff South
Kelvin Stevens
Ken Swift
Ryan Taylor
William Arthur Towers
R. Towlson
Kathy Turner
Norman Tyler
Alan Underwood
Terry Upton
Steve Westby
Paul Whitby
Alan Willett
Andy Williamson
Raymond Wilson (Gibralter)
Jon Wise